PENTECOST

PENTECOST
The Church Has Left the Building

Rob and Andy Frost
Edited by Mark Williamson

Authentic

MILTON KEYNES ● COLORADO SPRINGS ● HYDERABAD

14 13 12 11 10 09 08   7 6 5 4 3 2 1

First published 2008 by Authentic Media
9 Holdom Avenue, Bletchley, Milton Keynes, Bucks, MK1 1QR, UK
1820 Jet Stream Drive, Colorado Springs, CO 80921, USA
OM Authentic Media, Medchal Road, Jeedimetla Village, Secunderabad 500 055, A.P., India
www.authenticmedia.co.uk

Authentic Media is a division of IBS-STL U.K., limited by guarantee, with its Registered Office
at Kingstown Broadway, Carlisle, Cumbria CA3 0HA. Registered in England & Wales No.
1216232. Registered charity 270162

British Library Cataloguing in Publication Data
A catalogue record for this book is available from the British Library

ISBN: 978-1-85078-781-5

Cover Design by Huw Taylor
Print Management by Adare
Printed and bound in Great Britain by J.H. Haynes & Co., Sparkford

CONTENTS

FOREWORD
Ken Costa

Ken Costa is the Chairman of Alpha International, the organization which promotes the Alpha Course, and a Churchwarden of Holy Trinity Brompton. He has worked as an investment banker in the City of London for over thirty years (currently he is Chairman of Lazard International), and is the author of *God at Work*, an exploration of how the Christian faith should and can be lived out in day-to-day life at work.

Pentecost is the forgotten Christian festival. Like Christmas and Easter, it has, or at least used to have, an associated Bank Holiday. But unlike Christmas and Easter, the festival of the Spirit has largely been ignored by society. Christmas trees and carols, Easter bunnies and chocolates tell the world the Christmas and Easter stories. The marketing machines have not attempted to turn Pentecost into a secular fest.

So the field is clear for Pentecost to be shaped, to take its place as a central festival of the Christian year. There is a unique opportunity for Christians to celebrate life, originality, entrepreneurship, spirituality, newness and freshness, and in this way to showcase the inspirational work of the Spirit.

For many years I have longed to see this happen. But I never quite saw how it could be done. And then I heard that Rob Frost not only had a similar hope, but had actually done something about it by initiating what will become the Pentecost Festival.

This book, with its arresting call to leave the comfort zone of 'church', surveys the range and impact of the Spirit on the communities in which we live. It is a call to worship in action, a discovery of the empowering presence of the Spirit to unsettle us and to move us on – equipped and released to engage prophetically with a society losing its identity and longing for spiritual renewal. Nothing short of a new Pentecost is needed if we are to engage effectively with the issues that are now tearing apart the very fabric of our society.

But who will lead the way for this renewal of hope? I very much hope that this wonderful legacy project of Rob Frost, spearheaded by Andy Frost and his team, will lay down both a marker for Pentecost and a template that can be followed by many others.

The Spirit gives Life! What a slogan for our time. As we read this book and join in the Festival, we remind ourselves of the pulsating, invigorating, throbbing energy of the Spirit. This is the power which is there ready to be released to all those who wish to encounter the living God, to learn from him and to show his goodness to a broken world.

SLEEPLESS NIGHTS
Rob Frost

I landed in Los Angeles and managed to locate my car-rental centre, a bus ride across the huge airport complex. A twelve-hour flight, together with all the check-in security hassles at Heathrow and the usual immigration process at my 'port of entry' in the USA, had taken their toll. I was grateful that a representative of the convention I was speaking at was there to meet me, and even more relieved when she offered to sit beside me and navigate me through the complex network of Californian highways until at last I reached the country roads in the forests outside San Jose.

By the time I reached my log cabin deep in the midst of the redwood forest at the conference centre, I was absolutely exhausted. I didn't even unpack, but fell onto the bed and sank into a deep and satisfying sleep. This was, of course, a big mistake. I should have stayed awake and gently acclimatized to the local time zone, but when you're as tired as I was, nothing is sweeter than sleep. I knew I would pay for it the following night, and of course I did.

It must have been 4 a.m. when I woke with a start. It was very, very dark. Owls were hooting, and there was the eerie cry of a wild coyote somewhere in the distance. I was ravenous, and very much awake, so I opted for an 'early breakfast'. I rooted around the kitchen to find the generous supplies that my hosts had left for me, and I sat out on the veranda of my cabin with hot coffee and toast, and stared out at the moonlit outlines of the trees all around me.

It was as I sat there, in this rather bewildered state of 'jet-lag', that I felt God speak to me. Not as an audible voice, admittedly, but through a jolt of Holy Presence. The words came very clearly, almost as if they were sprayed onto the wall of my consciousness, graffiti-style. 'Why not organize an event that I'd like to come to?' he said. It shook me to the core.

Was this my imagination at work? Perhaps. Was it make-believe? Possibly. Could it have been real? It certainly felt real. And it certainly had a powerful effect on me. It was as if a surge of power had shot through my entire being. As if the things I had been struggling to come to terms with during the previous few months were now blindingly obvious. I felt that some kind of struggle was over, and some different course had been set for my future.

Of course, in order to understand the significance of this pre-dawn experience you'd need to know the context. I'd been the director of an event called Easter People since its launch twenty years previously, and I had recently announced that the next conference would be the last. There had been a lot of consultation, a plethora of 'forward planning papers', and a lot of discussion with my trustees and board. It wasn't a decision that we'd arrived at lightly; it had certainly been prayerfully submitted to the will of God.

The reasons for the closure were manifold. After peaking numerically in the year 2000, with 12,000-plus participants, the event had been in gentle decline ever since. The changes in school holiday dates were bound to have a detrimental effect on numbers over future years. The transfer of conference-centre management from town councils to large entertainment corporations had meant that rental prices had more than quadrupled. The event had become less and less cost effective.

Above all, however, those of us organizing it were feeling that it had passed its sell-by date. We knew that it would be hard to 're-launch' because so many wanted to keep it just the way it was! It was haemorrhaging money and staff resources from the rest of my ministry. This grew so serious that I began to feel as if I was raising large sums of money each year for mission, only to spend it on sustaining a loss-making Christian conference. But, above all, those of us at the centre of it were bored with the twenty-year merry-go-round of planning and preparation! It was a process which dominated the passing seasons of every year.

Having reached the point of 'laying down' Easter People, I was not looking for some other event to take its place! On the contrary, I was looking forward to developing a new style of ministry which gave me more time to speak and write, and which demanded far less 'organization' throughout the year!

On the twelve-hour journey to California I had thought about the future of my ministry again. Would anything ever replace Easter People, and if so, did I have a part to play in launching it? I submitted it all to Christ again, and as the carpet of white cloud slipped slowly past beneath us, I gave my ministry back to God as I had done so often down the years. God's faithfulness had been an undeniable experience throughout my life and I had no difficulty in recognizing that he would work his purposes out in the future, too.

On the veranda I chewed on my toast, and wondered what diverse manner of animal life was scurrying about in the shadowy forest ahead of me. The words wouldn't go away. 'Why not organize an event that I'd like to come to?' Had God actually spoken to me, or was this some subconscious echo from my prayers on the flight? I sincerely felt it was the former, but couldn't rule out the latter! But, whatever, the phrase intrigued me. What would an event that Jesus wanted to attend really look like?

I ambled back into the wooden cabin and picked up my airline carry-on case. I pulled out the biro and exercise book that I always carry on long-haul flights. I sank back into the veranda chair, and the warmth of the summer's night enveloped me. What would an event like this look like? What would make Jesus want to show up?

I knew in an instant what it didn't look like. And that shook me. I felt for sure that it wouldn't look 'religious'. It wouldn't be full of 'meetings' or 'seminars' . . . and it wouldn't be full of stressed-out Christians running from lecture to lecture, eager to mop up the latest teaching from the newest 'guru' on the block. It wouldn't just be lots of worship events, with a stream of eager praise bands each seemingly trying to outdo the others. And it wouldn't feature strutting preachers, some of whom seemed to be more intent on 'playing to the gallery' than prophetically challenging their hearers to the core.

Other negative images streamed across my mind. Long appeals for money. Uniformed guards stopping people from coming in. Fifteen-foot-high walls designed to keep out those not wearing the right wrist-band, badge or day-glow hand-stamp! And a great cloud of earnestness, of 'good intent' and glowing self-satisfaction – a kind of contemporary pietism that says to the world, 'I paid £1,000 to bring my family to this and we deserve a medal.' (They do, actually, because they could all have had a nice beach holiday in Tenerife for less!) No, I really couldn't see Jesus feeling comfortable here!

Would he turn up for an event with barely a black face in sight? Would he like it if the children were safely boxed into one space and the teens in another? Twenties in a trendy venue and the middle-aged in one with more comfortable seats, but all the ages never coming together? With the elderly made welcome only as long as they sang the latest songs? A middle-class constituency of decent people filling every seat, but no sign of the poor, the marginalized, the hurting or the downright peculiar?

And would he show up if there was no room for atheists, agnostics, cons, pimps, addicts, gays, divorcees, single mums, asylum seekers, Catholics, Muslims, Sikhs, sex workers and very lapsed Christians? I don't think so.

I finished my toast, took a last swig of coffee and began to write. The following three and a half hours flew by. I barely noticed the shadows receding and the orange glow of dawn filling the sky high above the tree-tops. It was a time of 'inspiration', when the flow of ideas moved so quickly that my pen could hardly keep up. The exercise book was practically full by the end of it.

I saw the event so clearly that it was as if I was there. It was as if the Body of Christ had woken up after a long sleep, and had discovered what fun it was to be alive in God.

I saw artists of every kind filling the streets. Big graffiti-style creations and fine oils on canvas. Great tapestries, and projects with lots of ordinary people 'having a go'. Telling God's story in pictures and symbols that anyone could understand.

I heard musicians, bands playing on the street corner, classical ensembles in shady city squares, and people singing. Gospel, barbershop, choirs and soloists, and young people rappin' in shop doorways. Praising God in a cacophony of beautiful harmony.

I smelt hot food drawing me towards a square filled with delicious tastings from all over the world. Rice and peas, curry, French fries, and big steaming silver bowls of Chinese food. The cultures of the world offering free food in celebration of the One who gave it. And in among it all there was dance, from ballet to contemporary, from liturgical to Latin, salsa, ballroom, street and hip-hop. A long conga was winding its way through the crowd. All celebrating the One who is Lord of the Dance of Life.

Somewhere in the distance church bells rang out the grandeur of God, and the roar of a crowd indicated that there was a football competition or sports tournament for inner-city kids not far away. Floating in on the gentle breeze was the sound of a theatre company in full swing, with laughter in the air. Round the corner a lorry appeared with a jazz band rockin' on its long trailer decking.

I passed a pub, and inside it a crowd of people were hearing eminent scientists debating the mysteries of the universe. In an up-market wine-bar three Christian politicians were debating the great challenges of the day in front of an audience who'd never seen anything like it. In a restaurant people were 'eating simply' as they discussed the ravages of world hunger. In a bookshop an audience was applauding a lecture on climate change.

People were streaming into a cinema to see a movie which told the greatest story. In a coffee-shop a Christian poet held the crowded tables in rapt attention. The sound of children laughing was emanating from a church schoolroom where puppets performed.

And there were churches with doors flung wide open. And inside were quiet spaces filled with flowers and beautiful music. A labyrinth of different things to see and do which were woven together into a liturgy of worship. And people from the street receiving bread and wine. And angelic faces, with the flow of fine oil running down their cheeks as they received faith-filled prayers for healing.

The most breath-taking aspect of this festival was its size. Everywhere I went the streets were full of life and colour and action and sound. And whatever I saw expressed something of the wonder and the power and the majesty of the Lord. It was more diverse than the Edinburgh Festival, culturally richer than Notting Hill Carnival, more cerebral than Malvern literature week, louder than Reading and more spiritual than Glastonbury. The sheer scale of it, the power of it, the joy of it, the wonder of it and the spirituality of it overwhelmed me.

But how could this be? I knew in an instant! It was just so obvious. This was the sleeping giant, the Church of Christ, slowly waking from its slumbers. If all the Christians in all the towns came together, just once, just for a day . . . and took to the streets to celebrate their God, what a difference they could make. If we could all lay down our denominational differences, put aside our theological squabbles, leave behind our different brands of churchmanship, and all do something together . . . what a sound we could make and what fun we could have!

And if every Christian agency stopped trying to sell us something, but instead, gave away their ministry for free. And if every denomination stopped their eternal conferencing and took to the streets to celebrate. And if the Pentecostals danced with the Reformed, and the Catholics sang with the Brethren, and the black churches prayed with the white, what a difference we could make.

I saw much more than this in my vision. Vast halls filled to capacity with crowds seeing all the very best that Christendom has to offer. Orchestras, and choirs, and bands, and theatre. And stadiums filled with prayer and praise. And worship that is truly a foretaste of the heavenly banquet.

And everywhere the ordinary people were saying, 'Is this Christianity? Is this Church? Are these believers?' For they had thought that the Church was dead. That Christianity was nothing more than the BBC's *Songs of Praise*. That belief had nothing to do with changing society. That Christians had nothing to give, and nothing to say. And in my heart I was seeing another Pentecost.

I closed my exercise book and went into my wooden cabin to shave. Soon I had to drive to San Jose airport to pick up my son, Andy, who was speaking at the youth meetings at the same convention as me. And when, finally, I met him striding through the arrivals area with his surfboard, I could see that he, too, was jet-lagged and exhausted.

The next morning at about 4 a.m. I woke with a start. I could smell the aroma of fresh coffee, and someone in the kitchen was making toast. I felt very hungry, so I got up. Andy turned to me and said, 'Care for an early breakfast, Dad?' Just as I had done the previous morning, we sat on the veranda together and looked out at the shadows among the trees.

'I've been thinking, Dad,' he said, 'about a new kind of event. Not a bit like Easter People. Something right outside the box. A place where everyone takes part, and not just the big-name speakers. . . .'

I ambled back to my room, picked up my exercise book, and returned to the veranda. 'Does it look anything like this?' I asked, and I started to read to him the outline I'd written twenty-four hours earlier.

'Yep. We're pretty much in the same ball-park,' said Andy. 'But where are you going to hold it?'

'That's the problem,' I replied. All day my mind had been turning over a list of market towns throughout the UK which might host such an event, but somehow nowhere felt right! I couldn't see how the event would ever fit into somewhere small, and if it was in a bigger city, I couldn't figure out how people would move from one location to another without getting exhausted along the way.

Andy smiled. 'It's got to be London. Right at the centre. Christians engaging with the arts, politics, science and entertainment where the action is. And people moving from location to location on the London Underground . . . the Northern Line. No problem!'

And so the journey to the Pentecost Festival began. It began with Andy and me, but already we have hundreds of fellow-travellers. I don't know if it's a journey we'll all complete! Since all this happened I've had a scary tryst with cancer which took my eye off the project for months, and we've met a fair few friends along the way who've poured cold water on the whole idea and told us how sure they are it'll never work!

But there have been others, many others, whose encouragement has been unstinting. In meetings with some of the best-known church leaders in the country we have felt deeply affirmed. They've assured us that Christians in the UK need to re-engage with society in a completely new way; that there's a desperate need for a 'signature event' which will show that Christianity is far from 'written off'. So far, twelve major Christian organizations have offered to co-sponsor the event, seeking to serve the 'greater good' rather than just the agenda of their own board. And what's surprised me most has been the encouragement of senior police officers, council officials, tourist board project managers and transport representatives who've all said, 'This is just what London needs.'

The phrase 'What would Jesus want to come to?' lives with me still. It is the mantra repeated at all our planning meetings; and it keeps us focused on the vision in hand. For, ultimately, the Person we want most to turn up is Jesus himself. We want to build something for him, and for his glory alone.

When the Spirit came at the first Pentecost he did two things. First, he empowered the very ordinary, scared and hesitant followers of Jesus with the fullness of God's Spirit. It was intensely personal, life-transforming and enabling. The Spirit turned them around, gave them gifts for service, and a personal experience of intimacy with God which showed them that what they believed was true. We need some more of that, for sure! And in many places throughout this Pentecost Festival, I hope that people will discover this fresh touch of God.

Secondly, he drove them out into the city square. He put them at the heart of a multi-faith and multi-cultural market-place, and gave them the power to speak in the language of the people. He gifted them to communicate in ways the people could understand, and in a manner that made them want a slice of the action themselves! Little wonder that 3,000 new believers were added to the Church that day!

The vivid reality of my two veranda breakfasts is still fresh in my mind. Whatever happens at the Pentecost Festival in London, I feel that it's a powerful word to the Church that is far more significant than just a couple of days in central London. It's a word that says that we have played the games of Christian conferencing for too long, we've built our little empires and developed our Christian subcultures. And I speak as one who has played his part in it, and who knows the game better than most.

But now God is calling us to receive the Spirit afresh and to do something different. It's a call to find a God-empowerment for all the people called Christian, and not just the 'big name' talent. It's a call to move out of our buildings, marquees, convention centres and 'conference facilities'. A call to take the action back into the multi-cultural marketplace, a call to celebrate what God has done in ways that shine with love and service.

This is not 'evangelism', with preachers shouting condemnation down loudspeaker horns. No, this is celebration! Let the party begin . . . and whoever wants to come is invited. Let's re-discover Pentecost.

POSTSCRIPT BY ANDY FROST

All these people were still living by faith when they died. They did not receive the things promised; they only saw them and welcomed them from a distance. . . .

Hebrews 11:13, NIV

It was a blustery November evening when Rob passed into eternity. His death was very sudden. The cancer had spread rapidly to his liver, but in those days where he lay between life and death, I had shown him the first draft of the Pentecost Festival programme. He lay there with wires wrapped around his body and breathing apparatus moving in time to each difficult breath.

As I sat on his bed showing him the programme, page by page, he responded with a barrage of exclamations: 'Marvellous! Excellent! This is going to be so good!' The vision we had received all those months ago, in a very different location and in very different health circumstances, was becoming reality.

It's sad to think that Rob will never see the Festival in his earthly life. Like Moses, he will not quite see the Promised Land. But as I re-read his chapter above, whilst my heart is still raw from the grief, the words jump off the page. Like a Joshua carrying the mantle, I carry this dream forward, helping this prophetic vision come to pass.

My father's death is a stark reminder that life is fragile. Let's make our lives count in glorifying Jesus.

BACK TO BASICS
Mark Williamson

I freely admit that I love the vision of the Pentecost Festival! It has been a pleasure to work alongside Rob and Andy, and be part of the unfolding story of God bringing the Festival to reality. I always broke out in an excited shiver whenever Rob brought us back to that beautiful word from God: 'I want you to organize an event that I would come to.' I still have a smile on my face now as I write those immortal words once more! I love the idea of celebrating and representing Jesus, and showing what the Church is all about, right in the heart of one of the most influential cities in the world.

I love it because although it's a fresh vision, it's actually a return to what the early Church was about. One of my favourite parts of the Bible is the first five chapters of Acts – the gripping story of how the kingdom of God broke out in Jerusalem and beyond in those first few years of the Church's life. Stories of passionate disciples who gave everything in following Jesus, and who therefore saw the Church 'turn the world upside down' (Acts 17:6, NLT).

I also love London. My work takes me all over the world, but more than any other prayer over the past five or maybe even ten years, I have constantly asked, 'Lord, please let your kingdom come in London.' I believe that whatever happens in London quickly influences the rest of the UK, so to see the kingdom grow in London would bless the Church around the nation. But wherever in the world I travel and see the Church growing and making an impact in society, I see a local church that is following the example of what the first Christians did during those first few chapters of Acts.

So let's look for a moment at what the early Church did out of that first Pentecost. After all, to truly celebrate Pentecost in the twenty-first century, we need to remember how Pentecost changed the world nearly 2,000 years ago. As I read those five chapters of Acts, I see five things that jump out. I see the importance of prayer, of the Holy Spirit, of unity, of community engagement, and of talking about Jesus.

These are values which are central to the Pentecost Festival, and they are values which can once again turn our world upside down for Jesus. They are also areas in which God has been stirring his Church in recent years, not only in the UK but around the world. As ever, he is the one going before us. . . .

Prayer

Prayer was central to the early Church. Five times within the first five chapters of Acts, it is specifically recorded as something the disciples did. After Jesus' ascension (but *before* the day of Pentecost) 'They all joined together constantly in prayer, along with the women and Mary the mother of Jesus, and with his brothers' (Acts 1:14, NIV). Prayer was not something left to one or two people to carry out. All 120 of the current believers met together to pray, whether they were young or old, male or female, old believers or new converts.

They prayed before casting lots to determine Judas' replacement (Acts 1:24). After 3,000 were added to their numbers following Peter's first sermon, they all 'devoted themselves . . . to prayer' (2:42, NIV). Later, we read of Peter and John 'going up to the temple at the time of prayer' (3:1, NIV). They prayed with their new Christian brothers, but they also did not neglect the traditional Jewish times and forms of prayer they had grown up with. And then when Peter and John returned the next day with the story of how they had been arrested, imprisoned and threatened by the Jewish leaders, the whole fledgling Christian community 'raised their voices together in prayer to God' (4:24, NIV).

What do we learn from this? Two things stand out for me. They prayed *constantly*. Not for them simply a one-off laying things before God. Prayer was the last resort, but also the first response and the regular practice for this band of radical disciples. They prayed, and they prayed, and they kept on praying. And then they prayed some more. They also prayed *corporately*. No doubt they each also had times alone with God, as Jesus had modelled for them, but they knew the value of praying together as a community.

We need to recapture their fervency and seriousness of prayer if we want to also 'turn the world upside down' as they did. God is already raising up a new prayer movement around the world. We see this through the growing momentum of initiatives such as 24–7 Prayer and the Global Day of Prayer, as well as the countless local churches who have begun praying with renewed determination. But we need to do more. The first disciples prayed solidly for ten days between the ascension of Jesus and the outpouring of the Holy Spirit. What would happen if we did the same? Abandoned everything else for ten days of solid prayer? Perhaps then there truly would be a second Pentecost. . . .

What did the disciples pray for? We know they prayed for God's direction for themselves, and for his hand to guide events (e.g. when electing Matthias); and we know they prayed for boldness, anointing and power as they talked with people about Jesus (Acts 4:29–30). But no doubt they also knew the simple truth that prayer was one of the best means for drawing closer to God, so they prayed simply because they hungered after him. We need more of this sort of prayer.

When we pray, God works. When we don't pray, he doesn't work. It really is that simple. We need to pray, constantly and corporately, for God's direction and anointing, in all we do. If we pray like this, in fervent groups, for weeks, months and years, what will God not do?! In my local church a small group of us have begun praying together every Sunday evening for God to bring people to know him in our little corner of south-west London. I don't fully know how or when God will answer such prayers, but I'm excited because I *know* that he will do so in some amazing way. Every powerful movement of God throughout history has been preceded by a group of people faithfully praying, sometimes for days, sometimes for years. Will you be a part of such a group?

The Holy Spirit

The early Church story is really a story of the Holy Spirit. He is the one doing everything. He is always the centre of the narrative. The only reason we cannot label him the hero of the story is because he always points us back towards Jesus, the true hero of the Church. He comes to help us testify to Jesus, and no one else. But he is central to all that happens for good in the first five chapters of Acts. Without him the early Church could do nothing. It's unsurprising, then, that he is mentioned sixteen times in these five momentous chapters!

In line with the prayers of the early Church, the Spirit's twin roles in the story are to provide direction for the apostles, and to provide empowerment for their work.

With regard to direction, it is a great irony that the last recorded action of the disciples before the Spirit came was to elect a replacement for Judas Iscariot through casting lots. Just a few days later at Pentecost the Holy Spirit came upon them in a powerful new way, and the days of casting lots were forever over! No longer did they have to resort to such methods to determine the will of God – they had his very presence guiding them for all such issues. Before making important decisions we too should ask God which direction he wants us to take, and be expectant that the Spirit will speak to us. We need to be listening to him, and be open to hearing in whatever way he chooses to speak to us. Our God is a communicative, relational God! He is always speaking to us. The question usually is, are we listening?

As well as guiding, the Spirit also empowered them for all they were called to do. During his trial, Peter is specifically described as being 'filled with the Holy Spirit' (Acts 4:8, NIV) – it was not his words but God's words that he was uttering. The Spirit can and wants to empower us for all of the actions we do in life, and if only we invite him in, he will often do 'immeasurably more than all we ask or imagine' (Eph. 3:20, NIV).

I can remember one occasion when I was preaching in my local church, and twice I found myself making unplanned references to Buddhism, comparing various aspects of it to Christianity, showing how it had a certain logic but was lacking essentially in *life*. It is a religion that teaches one to die to self, but then cannot replace self with any new life. Only afterwards did I learn that someone in the congregation had been seriously considering Buddhism as a way of life over the past few weeks. The Holy Spirit anointed my words so that they spoke personally to him. Such things should and can be everyday occurrences for us, whether we fully understand what is going on or not. The Holy Spirit can anoint us to preach and to pray, but also to drive a car, design a building or cut someone's hair. There is nothing (sin excepted) that God does not want to be a part of in our lives; he wants to share it all with us, guiding and empowering us within it.

We, in the early twenty-first century, are experiencing a pouring out of the Holy Spirit unprecedented since the times of the early Church. We see this in the charismatic movements which have affected all parts of the Church, but also in the countless ways in which Christians and non-Christians alike are becoming more aware of spirituality, and are looking and hungering more for the presence of God in their lives. As God continues to pour out his Spirit across the world, we move closer to once again living through times of true Pentecost. But do we hunger after God like the early Church did? And do we seek his direction and anointing as regularly as they did?

Unity

The early disciples were united together in ways without parallel for the Church of today. We read that they 'devoted themselves . . . to the fellowship . . . . All the believers were together and had everything in common. Selling their possessions and goods, they gave to anyone as he had need' (Acts 2:42–44, NIV). Later we hear that 'All the believers were one in heart and mind' (4:32, NIV). They prayed together, they ate together, and they shared all they had with each other. And partly because there were no factions amongst them, 'they were highly regarded by the people' (5:13, NIV). Even the story of Ananias and Sapphira from chapter 5 casts a reflection back to unity. In a direct comparison with the previous story of Barnabas, who had sold a field and given the proceeds over to the apostles, this couple sold a property but kept back some money for themselves, and then lied to the apostles about what they had done. Whenever we formally break with another wing of the Church, or even when we personally may lie to another Christian, as Ananias and Sapphira did here, we bring one more painful break to the Body of Christ.

This importance of unity is found throughout the Bible. In Psalm 133 David exclaims: 'How good and pleasant it is when brothers live together in unity. . . . For there the LORD bestows his blessing, even life for evermore' (verses 1, 3, NIV). God brings eternal life where there is unity! Not on the Christians already working in unity, since they already have eternal life by virtue of being those who already know Christ. The eternal life he bestows will be on those the united Church is reaching out to. When we reach out to others in unity, God promises us results! Small wonder, then, that Jesus prayed for the unity of his Church on the night before his death: 'I pray also for those who will believe in me through their message, that all of them may be one. . . . May they be brought to complete unity to let the world know that you sent me' (John 17:20–23, NIV).

The world instinctively knows the truth of the above statement. To paraphrase: 'When the Church acts in unity, the world will recognize that

Jesus was sent by the Father.' On numerous short-term mission trips that I have been involved with, when we talk with people outside the Church, the first response is invariably: 'Wow – it's wonderful that you've got the churches working together.' And people are far more interested in listening to the message of a united Church than a divided Church. When local churches stop competing and start co-operating with each other, local people start taking notice.

There is also a practical consideration in all of this. I have seen a church with forty members want to do something for the teenagers hanging around in the graveyard, but struggle to put on a regular youth club due to the smallness of their congregation. Then they realized that if they worked with the three other churches in the same village, they would suddenly have four times the people-power. And since God loves unity amongst his followers, he will bless that united group of Christians with an anointing greater than that of any one single group trying to go it alone. 'There the LORD bestows his blessing – even life for evermore.'

There is a growing sense of the importance of unity and ecumenism in the Church around the world. We are gradually realizing that no one group, church or denomination can succeed on its own. It is when we work together that we truly become the Body of Christ. As one person, group, church or denomination, we are simply an eye, a nose, an ear, or a leg. *Together* we each become a part of the whole. The growing unity of local churches has been seen in recent years through united missions such as Festival Manchester, SOULINTHECITY, Merseyfest and NE1 in our big cities. These saw local churches working together in mission on unprecedented levels. And not only that, but they also saw the parachurch organizations working alongside them. For too long there has been division and competition between local church and parachurch, and also between parachurch organizations themselves. When such organizations also start to co-operate with each other, and begin again to serve local churches rather than leaching resources away from them, we will be moving ever closer to the sort of unity Jesus desires and prays for in his followers, and his blessing will consequently not be far away.

Is your church working in unity with the others in your local town? Or do you see each other as the competition? Are you working with the many Christian agencies out there who could support you, or are you trying to go it alone?

Community engagement

The early Church knew the importance of fellowship, of worship, of prayer, of good teaching, and of the sacraments (Acts 2:42–47) – of meeting together to perform sacred acts. But they did not neglect the importance of serving their local community with the love of Jesus. They were proactive in helping to meet the needs of first-century Judean society, earning such a reputation for healing that 'people brought the sick into the streets and laid them on beds and mats so that at least Peter's shadow might fall on some of them as he passed by' (Acts 5:15, NIV). All of their healing of people, just like that in the ministry of Jesus, was motivated by true love for the people they were serving, and it met people at an area of great need.

There are many needs in society today which the Church is concerned about. All of the chapters in this book, written by partners of the Pentecost Festival, are filled with real-life stories of how different aspects of the Church are engaging with real issues that are of concern to all members of our global or local communities, both Christian and non-Christian alike. They are included here to tell the story of how the Church is indeed trying to still walk in the ways of that historic Pentecost nearly 2,000 years ago. They are also included to inspire you with ideas as to what your local branch of the universal Church can do to engage with society, and continue playing its part in the great work of kingdom building in every village, town and city on the planet.

Communicating Jesus

Talking about Jesus was the obsessive passion of the early Church. Whether the disciples were hauled before the Sanhedrin, healing people on the streets, teaching in the temple, or just going to a friend's house for a meal, 'they never stopped teaching and proclaiming the good news that Jesus is the Christ' (Acts 5:42, NIV). They used every opportunity they had to talk about Jesus. They showed how he was relevant to every area of life, and to every person they encountered.

We in the twenty-first century seem to have lost their ability to tell people about Jesus. This is such an important issue that the next chapter is dedicated to it. But each of the later chapters written by our Festival partners also shows in different ways how the Church is really representing Jesus to the world at large.

The Pentecost Festival

Prayer, the Holy Spirit, unity, community engagement and communicating Jesus. The Pentecost Festival seeks to connect with all these strands of what God is and has been doing since that first Pentecost until now. It's time for us to get back to basics, and follow more intently the example which the early Church has given us.

Linking with the Global Day of Prayer, and encouraging people to pray throughout all we do, we hope to continue in the upsurge of prayer happening across society.

We hope to be a place where the Holy Spirit longs to come down and bless with his manifest presence all that happens in connection with the Festival, and we are confident he is the one who has gone before us, guiding us into this current place.

We hope to promote unity within the Church through bringing together many cultures, races, local churches, denominations, and parachurch organizations in celebration of Jesus.

We hope to showcase all the positive engagement the Church is involved in around the world, whilst also engaging in practical and loving ways with the people of London and beyond during the Festival weekend.

And in all this we hope to communicate to every person we meet the great Person of Jesus Christ himself.

Ultimately, we hope that the Festival will indeed be the sort of event that Jesus would want to come to. It is all about him, it is all for him, and it is all a representation of who he is, for the rest of the world to see.

REPRESENTING JESUS
Andy Frost

'Sir, pull down your pants!' said the US airport customs officer.

A bemused look fell across Rich's face as his eyes desperately searched for confirmation. He was silent and stood motionless as the officer again barked his order in a stern American accent coupled with a tense look of authority.

The queue of holiday-makers and business-people wrapped itself around the airport departures check-in. Rich was holding up the line and impatience grew in the bulging queue waiting their turn to gingerly march through the metal detector. The restless queue had their eyes focused on Rich as the officer, with a raised and uncompromising tone, said one final time, 'Pull down your pants – now!'

So Rich did exactly what the officer asked. With the queue of commuters looking on, Rich seized the top of his underwear and began to pull down his trousers and boxers in one swift action – publicly revealing more than the customs officer could ever possibly want to see.

The officer's look of authority morphed into a look of distinct panic as he gasped, 'What are you doing?'

Rich was thrown and looked particularly vulnerable. 'You told me to pull down my pants!' he replied awkwardly.

'Pull them up! Pull them up!' was the officer's urgent appeal as he turned his head, looking away in disgust.

In one swift moment an unexpected scenario had revealed the simplest of language barriers between American English and British English. When Brits use the word 'pants' we mean 'underpants', but when an American customs officer uses the word 'pants', he definitely means 'trousers'.

One of the most basic and complex issues that humankind has to grapple with is communication. Communication can be one of the simplest of devices. Children quickly learn to communicate the most basic of needs for warmth, food and affection with cries and simple movement. As we progress along the conveyor-belt of life, we learn to communicate our opinions, our hopes, our fears, our emotions. . . .

The word 'communication' means more than how we, as individuals, interact. Communication is a multi-billion-dollar industry, as high-street brands and political parties alike hire PR gurus to sell more than just a product or a policy, but lifestyles and values. And when communication is badly handled it can lead to bankruptcy, civil unrest, or on an international level, world war.

Communication is important.

And when it comes to communication, perhaps the Church has a problem. Perhaps the Church has forgotten how to communicate. And this is a serious issue, when we hold the most important message of all.

We have the life-changing news of the cross. We have victory over death. We have a living relationship with our Father in heaven. We have life in all its fullness. We have every spiritual blessing. We have the Spirit of God at work in our lives. We have hope. We have truth. We have love.

Yet as I meet people who have no Christian faith, they have rarely received this message from the Church. They regurgitate newspaper headlines about church controversies over issues of sexuality. They share their experiences of boring baptismal services. They explain how all Christians are hypocrites who say one thing and do another. They see the Church as a historic institution with 'nice' old people who like making jam. They believe that there is nothing relevant that the Church has to speak into their lives today. And when I meet these people and hear their opinions, it breaks my heart.

We have an urgent message of relevance that can transform individuals, cities and countries. A message so radical, that at times in history it has been considered by those in power as 'dangerous'. And it is vital that we re-discover how to communicate it today!

The Church has not always had a communication problem.

At the first Pentecost, the Spirit of God moved and the disciples were catapulted out of the upper room and into the public places. They preached Jesus' message of life and 3,000 people chose to accept it. God moved in the public places.

The Spirit of God came not just to give the early disciples a warm fuzzy sensation in their worship times, but to transform them into bold witnesses who live in the world. When it comes to communication, it is vitally important that we, like the early disciples, are where people are at – in public places where we can communicate this scandalous message of grace.

Sometimes we are guilty of waiting in our church buildings, expecting that one day people will just start coming back to our church meetings. Sometimes we think that if we just change our organ for a worship band, or if we serve better coffee, or if we just buy a top-of-the-range projector, then people will flock to join us on a Sunday morning.

But the disciples did not wait for people to come to them in the upper room. They took Jesus to the public places. Their faith was not concealed behind closed doors – it erupted into the streets of Jerusalem, unleashing revival and rioting!

Party time

I like going to parties. Jesus appears to be keen on them too. Last week I went a party that was full of hedonists – searching for the next pleasurable experience. I felt slightly out of place, as the people around me were swapping stories of heavy drug-induced nights and boasting of sexual exploits. Meanwhile I embarked on an evening of 'polite conversation'.

The polite conversation routine normally begins with a probing question along the lines of 'Why are you here this evening?' It's a great opener with plenty of scope as you search for common ground on which you can base a good conversation. You may have friends, places or interests in common. But when the opener finds no footing, the second question is, usually without fail, 'And what do you do for a living?'

The short, dark-haired lady tilted her head to one side quizzically as she asked me this question. She was wearing a tatty old rock T-shirt and a black leather strap around her neck. Her eyes seemed to study my face and, in an instant, I felt quite awkward.

I had just a moment to work out how to phrase, 'I am an evangelist.' Not always easy – especially in the throws of a hedonistic party. There are ways of dumbing it down, and I quickly skimmed through the filing cabinet in my head for possible answers: 'I am a . . . youth worker, an entrepreneur, an event organizer, a charity worker'?

What I actually said was: 'I work for the Church.'

Thoroughly expecting an adverse reaction, it almost felt as if I was making a confession – my confession being that I want to see lives transformed as people interact with Jesus. Preparing to be gunned down with sarcastic comments, I followed up with, 'What do you think of that?'

'What, really?' came the response.

A barrage of questions followed. Questions about sex, about 'being religious', about life, about death, about church, about reality. . . . The conversation ended as she shared *her* confession – her confession being that she deeply desired some kind of faith in God.

Something is surely wrong in our world when people are so caught up with 'fitting in' that they have no space to confess that they desire to know God.

I find myself in this scenario regularly – chatting to people who have no faith. Frequently they say to me, 'I have never met a real life Christian before.' Their concept of the Christian faith is caricatured by Dawn French and President Bush.

To communicate to the world, we need to take our church communities to the masses. People want to understand, they want to get their heads around the deeper questions of life, and we can't afford to wait behind our stained-glass windows any longer. We need to be where the people are at.

Maybe we need to take our home groups into the local pub or into Starbucks.

Maybe we need to take our prayer meetings to the streets and the hospitals.

Maybe we need to make our mission-field not just some distant land, but our work-place.

Maybe we need to move our church community back into the neighbourhood.

We often wonder what happened to this dangerous adventure of faith that the early followers of Jesus were called to. The truth is that when we live in the safety of our meetings, we can easily forget to 'Go'.

If we really want to communicate the Gospel message and to see it impact people's lives, we must step outside into that big, bad world. We must be prepared for events that will mess up the way we see church working, and that challenge our understanding of God. We must be prepared for things that will shock us and hurt us. But when we step into the public places, fuelled by the Spirit of God, the Great Commission becomes reality and the adventure begins.

Speaking to the tribes

But communication is more than just being in public places. It's also about what we do before we get there and when we get there.

At Pentecost, the disciples 'began to speak in other tongues'. As they began to speak, they were labelled as being intoxicated. A crowd quickly gathered. And then the crowd responded, 'We hear them declaring the wonders of God in our own tongues!'

What an amazing experience this must have been for the Jews who had gathered in Jerusalem for Pentecost from many nations. Something unique was happening and they could not help but get caught up in it! The disciples were unable to keep quiet about 'the wonders of God'.

We can easily get distracted from what we are trying to communicate. We are not trying to communicate a perfect theology. We are not attempting to communicate merely good morals. We are not striving to communicate church tradition. What we need to be communicating is simply Jesus, and the opportunity to enter into a relationship with the Living God.

In order to keep being effective, we need to keep our eyes focused on the real Jesus. Not some moral, bearded, nice guy, but the Son of God who had authority. Authority to calm storms. Authority to heal the sick and raise the dead. Authority to challenge injustice. Authority to protect the marginalized. Authority to love. Authority over death. And it is with this authority that he sends us into the world.

Sometimes I think we forget that this is the Jesus we are trying to communicate. His life, his death and his resurrection are the message. And it is in relationship with him that we discover more of Jesus. It was in the upper room, as the disciples waited and prayed, that they connected with God on a whole new level. This kind of prayerful relationship needs to be the fuel for our communication.

In the years that I have spent in local church leadership, it seems clear to me that one of the key factors in effective mission is prayer. It is in prayer that our perspectives are changed. We look up and discover afresh 'the wonders of God'. And when we discover these wonders, it is hard to stay quiet. It is when we are overwhelmed by 'the wonders of God' in the public places, that we can begin to share Jesus.

We live in a society bubbling with different tribes and tongues. As Jerusalem was full of different people groups, so the same is true today. There are so many subcultures, ranging from the urban hip-hop-ers, to the suited and booted City bankers, to the football fans who travel the country religiously following their team. Each culture has its own language. A language which is more than mere words. A language which dictates dress, values, behaviour . . . a language which allows people to belong.

As we spill out of our church buildings, it is important that we communicate the message of Jesus to these subcultures. The message does not change, but the way in which we reveal it has to show its relevance. And if we are going to communicate to the culture, we need to listen to what the culture is saying.

A church that I pass regularly has a luminous pink sign that states in big, black letters: 'Jesus is the Answer!' This sign, for me, sums up something of the communication issue that we have. We tell the world that the answer is Jesus, but we have rarely taken the time to discover the question.

It is vital in all communication that we listen. We need to listen to the questions that lie behind the lifestyles of today. That means moving into deeper conversations with the hairdresser and the shop assistant. That means engaging with the books and the blogs that people are reading and the movies people are watching.

I have given seminars at various events over the years about connecting with culture. I frequently gather a bundle of mainstream magazines and ask Christians to find articles, advertising and pictures that identify some of the underpinning questions that people are dealing with. Generally the Christians are shocked by the content – by the graphic depictions of contemporary lifestyles.

But as the groups probe deeper, they begin to find common questions asked in the subcultures of today. One of the common questions that arises is: 'Do you love me?' There is this desperate search for acceptance and belonging.

As we enter the public places, I often find that many people are turned off when we start by preaching Jesus. But when we listen to the questions that they are asking, they open up to hear something of what we have to say.

As the disciples entered the public places in Jerusalem all those years ago, they understood the question that was on everybody's lips. The Passover had been celebrated seven weeks earlier, and as they gathered they were asking, 'Where is our Messiah?' It was into that context that Peter preached Jesus the Christ.

That same message would not have been understood in today's context. Peter and the disciples were speaking to a specific audience who had a belief in God but did not understand how Jesus fitted into the equation. To preach the Gospel today, we must understand our twenty-first-century audience.

I regularly share the Gospel with young people, and I have learnt how important it is to understand their context. When I focus a Gospel presentation on eternal life, they switch off. Many young people have no connection with death and rarely think about it. They often feel they are immortal and can wait to make a decision on eternal life until they are in their sixties. But when I speak about having a 'full life' their eyes light up, and I am able to share this promise of Jesus.

Lesslie Newbigin writes:

If the gospel is to be understood; if it is, as we may say, 'to make sense' then it has to be communicated in the language of those to whom it is addressed and it has to be clothed in signs and symbols which are meaningful to them. . . . Those to whom it is addressed must be able to say, 'Yes, I see.'

It is as we listen that we learn how best to communicate. As the disciples preached in 'different tongues', so we must speak in different languages to different subcultures.

Many people hold tight to the concept that the Church is boring, hypocritical and judgemental. As a result, people have been turned off Jesus. But perhaps it is time that the Church rediscovered how to *represent*

Jesus so that we might *present* him once we have won the opportunity to share. We need to represent the Jesus who listens, who cares for the poor, who has compassion, who laughs, who weeps, who empowers, who stands for justice, who loves creativity, who offers life.

This means representing him not just with our words, but also with our lives. This means getting our hands dirty. This means listening. This means living generously. This means laughing with those who are rejoicing and weeping with those who are mourning. This means taking more risks. This means standing up against the injustice in the world, even though it may threaten our comfortable lives. We need to represent this Jesus of unconditional love.

In the chapters that follow we can see new ways in which the Church is connecting with people on so many different levels. From gun crime, to world poverty, to comedy, to the arts, we are able to represent something more of this wonderful Jesus. As we represent Jesus, crowds gather and we have the opportunity to present the real Jesus. What a staggering challenge those first disciples leave for us today!

God is already at work. God is already planting questions in the hearts of this nation. It is time for us, as the Church, to wake up. Let's allow God to remind us of his wonders. Let's leave the safety of our comfort zones. Let's represent Jesus. And when we do this, let's take the opportunities we will find ourselves in to daily communicate Jesus.

Wess Stafford

REPRESENTING
THE COMPASSIONATE
JESUS

Let the little children come to me,
and do not hinder them,
for the kingdom of heaven
belongs to such as these.
Matthew 19:14, NIV

Wess Stafford is President and CEO of Compassion International, an organization fighting poverty around the world by sponsoring children in developing nations. By doing this they represent the compassionate Jesus.

Getting at the root

If we are going to strike poverty at its root, we must take aim at this condition called fatalism. This is what keeps people penniless, sick, ignorant, vulnerable, oppressed, and without God.

I know this is perhaps a different perspective on poverty than you have typically heard. Most people see only the circumstances and conditions. But poverty is an inside-out issue. It does its greatest damage on the inside, where it often cannot be seen.

Don't get me wrong; when it comes to the poor, I believe it is 'good to do good'. But not all good is of equal value or is strategic enough to attack poverty at its core and reverse its deadly effect. If we are going to do good, why not also be strategic? Henry Ford once said about the poor, 'The only thing you can give a man without hurting him is an opportunity.' He knew that no amount of handouts or doing good things on a person's behalf gets to the heart of the matter, which is the inner, destructive message of 'Just give up.' An opportunity, on the other hand, cuts to the very core by saying, 'I believe in you! You can do it. Don't you dare give up!'

Think of a grapevine that consistently produces sour, bitter grapes. Nobody wants to eat them. What should be done about this? I suppose it would be a good thing (at least better than doing nothing) to pick off the destructive, bad fruit and throw it away. It feels good to do that. You feel like you're making a difference.

But the next season, the same bad fruit will be back – maybe even more of it. This will go on season after season until someone finally decides to get at the underground sewage system that is causing the bitter fruit. Only then will this grapevine become useful, producing the sweet fruit you would expect.

On the bitter vine of poverty are all kinds of sour fruit. Poor housing. Contaminated water. Injustice. Economic limitations. A harsh environment. Lack of infrastructure. Poor health. War. But these are not poverty. They are merely its symptoms. They are deplorable and should be addressed by caring people. But the mere elimination of poverty's symptoms will never win the war.

We should have learned this lesson long ago in the United States. Some thirty-five years ago I myself was deeply and passionately engaged as a young student at Moody Bible Institute. Chicago's Juvenile Court put me to work as a community aide in the most deplorable ghetto of the city, Cabrini Green. My fellow students and I worked hard at tutoring and befriending at-risk children. All around us, big government programmes were addressing everything but the human element at the core of the problem.

Sadly, today the high-rise housing of Cabrini Green, the basketball courts, and lighted parking lots are being torn down. They didn't work. Poverty didn't get defeated. The violence, crime, hatred, and hunger persisted. More than three decades have come and gone, and we have lost another entire generation! That is because deep in the ground of such deplorable conditions, at the base of the bitter grapevine, the roots of poverty keep producing the same destructive results year after year.

Albert Einstein once defined insanity as 'doing the same thing over and over again and expecting different results'. The battle against poverty has fallen into this trap more than a few times.

Several years after the Cabrini Green experience, I was doing my doctoral studies at Michigan State University. By this time I had seen more than my share of poverty and its destructiveness, in the lives of West Africans and in Haitians. I sat through one graduate course after another analyzing the various aspects, causes, conditions, and strategies to address poverty from the perspective of many experts, bilateral and multilateral organizations, and governments.

Once in a while I would annoy and challenge my fellow students by leaning back in my chair and saying, 'I still say that the most loving and strategic thing that can be done for children in poverty is to bring them to their heavenly Father.'

They would groan and reply, 'Ah, Wess, there you go putting a spiritual Band-Aid on the hurts of the world!' They sounded really informed and knowledgeable with their dismissal of my perspective.

I'd just smile and say, 'Yeah, you got a problem with that?' After a good-hearted laugh, I would explain that when you understand poverty's root, its core, as a destructive mind-set that says, 'I don't matter. There is nothing special about me. Why should I try? Why should I dare to hope? Who cares about me?' – you have stumbled right into the very heart of the Gospel. Every Christian who has experienced the love of God in his or her life is in a perfect place to understand the centrality of this perspective.

Sometimes when I speak with pastors, I find them a little bit hesitant or awkward with this whole issue of poverty. *Is it within our mandate?* They wonder. What about the struggle between spiritual and physical? Is it part of their discipleship calling?

I tell them that nobody is in a better position than they to understand the very root of poverty or to champion the most strategic path out of it. When a poor child comes to understand that God Almighty, maker of heaven and earth, knows her name, that God cares deeply about her, that he knows how many hairs are on her head, that he etched the unique design of her fingerprints, that he gave her a unique and delightful way of laughing, and that he sent his own Son to die on the cross to save her, that leads to an epiphany that changes everything. 'I guess I matter after all!'

When a child in poverty says, 'I matter,' he has just taken the first teetering step out of poverty! The outer circumstances with which he struggles may not have changed at all, but the inner core, the root of his personhood, is vastly altered. The healing can now begin, from the inside out.

How? The child begins to think, 'Well, if I matter, what I think matters, and what I feel is valid and important.' This step enables a child to leave some of the worst abuse behind. No longer will the little girl in Bangkok acquiesce to selling her precious body for a few dollars to any pervert on the street. A sense of value has been regained.

When a child in a Compassion project gets to this important stage in personal development, he or she is surrounded by caring people of the Church and the consistent message, 'That's right, sweetheart. You *do* matter. So tell me, what do you think? What do you feel? Here, can you paint it for me on this easel? Can you play it on this guitar? Can you sing it for me? Can you write it in a letter to your sponsor?' Day after day, week after week, this awakening moves consistently and lovingly forward. The twinkle, that almost-extinguished sparkle, reappears in the child's eyes. His or her posture straightens up. Confidence is restored. That long-lost smile and that desire to give a hug or trustingly hold your hand slowly blossom like a flower. Mom and Dad start to notice, and joy fills their faces.

As the years pass, they experience success upon success. A well-drawn picture. Applause for a beautiful dance. Getting from first grade to second after passing a difficult exam. A pat on the back when their soccer or volleyball team excels. The blue ribbon for Scripture memory or a tapestry well done.

Faraway sponsors watch their progress over the years and join in the applause and affirmation of the children's progress. It's magic to watch!

Then comes a day, usually in adolescence, when the youth will look you in the eye, straighten their shoulders, and say, 'You want to know what I think and feel? I'll tell you!' (This may come in the form of an essay, a speech to the community, or a quiet conversation under the mango tree.) They look around at their surroundings and say boldly, 'I don't think my community should look like this.' Or they see an injustice or cruelty and say, 'I don't think it's right that people treat each other that way.' Eventually they'll say, 'See what's going on over there? That's wrong – and I can fix it!'

The immediate response of the caring adult is, 'You know what? I think you're absolutely right! You could do that. Go fix it. Make your world a better place!' At such a wonderful moment, a productive life is launched. Now the adult's role is to watch, help, and applaud.

It all begins, I maintain, with that powerful and under-utilized thing called love. God's love for the individual is displayed by those people who reflect his love in their words and deeds. It ultimately gets understood and accepted by the child in poverty, and through that individual's love for others, the world gets changed.

One changed child eventually changes a family. A changed family will influence change in its church. Enough changed churches will transform the community. Changed communities change regions. Changed regions will in time change an entire nation.

The runner

This, my friends, is the path out of poverty! And it happens one child at a time. I know that has become a cliché, but it is absolutely true if you understand that poverty, an overwhelming global tragedy, occurs one life at a time. It destroys lives one at a time. And it is defeated one life at a time.

Curiously enough, the poor seem to know this instinctively. All over the world I've found that if you ask a poor man or woman, 'What can I do to help you?' the answer is the same. It doesn't matter whether you're in Asia, Africa, or Latin America, conversing in Tagalog, Lingala, or Spanish. Whatever the circumstance, the poor do *not* request money or personal things. They invariably look back at you with hopeful eyes and say, 'If you want to help me, help my children.'

If throughout this chapter you have discounted my passion by saying to yourself, 'Well, Wess Stafford is a sentimentalist toward children; he's the kind of guy who gets all mushy around little kids,' let me tell you, it's a lot more than sentiment. I truly believe in this cause for hard-nosed, objective, strategic reasons. I'm not just looking to feel good or assuage my conscience. I believe this is the *smart* way to combat the poverty problem.

Notice, I didn't say the *fast* way. The child-centred strategy takes several years to produce fruit. It's not as quick as whipping out your cheque-book and changing an external condition in a poor neighbourhood. But it is a lot more permanent. It gets results that will last.

Some approaches to poverty are microwave solutions. I'm talking instead about a crock-pot approach. It may take longer, but the taste at the end of the day is far better and the food more nutritious. It feeds the soul.

So there is something for everyone to do. We who know God's love and have some money in our pockets can reach out to lift up the child in poverty. That child, once awakened to his or her value to God, proceeds to change the local circumstances. It is not an either/or. The responsibility is not entirely on one set of shoulders or the other. We work together.

I come back to my premise that merely addressing the circumstances and conditions of poverty at the community level is not enough. There are simply too many corrupt levels of society for benefit to 'trickle down' to the neediest. It just doesn't work – or at least not often enough to make it worth my life's effort! But when the poorest of the poor are the ones changed, they come alive and 'bubble up' through their community. That breaks the back of poverty and brings a sustainable transformation, by transformed people, that cannot be taken away. While changed circumstances sometimes change people, changed people always change circumstances.

One of my favourite stories of the power of child sponsorship didn't happen in the realm of my organization; it was some other effort whose name I have lost. But to me, it epitomizes the wonderful power of a concerned adult to change a child's life. In this case, it was a British school-teacher who sometime around 1970 began to sponsor a little boy in Kenya. Every month she sent her modest cheque. But she did more than that. This teacher understood child development, and she could tell right away by his early letters that he was trapped in hopelessness.

'Dear Sponsor,' he wrote in the beginning. 'Here is a picture of me. You can see that I am not very handsome.'

His British sponsor smiled warmly and wrote back: 'I think you are wrong about that. I have your picture on my desk. I look at you every day, and I think you are very handsome.'

The next letter from Kenya said, 'Well, thank you, but you can see from my report card they sent you that I'm not very smart. I'm so sorry.'

Again she smiled. 'Well, I promise you that you are as smart as God wants you to be to do whatever he wants you to do,' she wrote back. 'Just do your very best!'

In time this little boy began to sense that his sponsor actually believed in him and was committed to him. He was eight years old when he sat down and wrote, 'Guess what I just learned? I discovered that I can run faster than anyone else in my classroom. There are five of us, and I am the fastest!'

Knowing how important the taste of success is to any child, but especially to a child living in poverty, the woman wrote back, 'Well, it is good to be good at something. I'm proud of you. Be the best runner you can be!'

The little boy listened to her and began to run. A few years later a letter came that said, 'Guess what? I now run faster than anyone in my whole school!'

Her reply came a few weeks later. 'Wow! That is really something! I am so proud of you. Keep on running and be the best you can be!'

The years of their friendship rolled by. The woman retired from teaching and settled into a little cottage in the south of England. Meanwhile, the lad remembered her words of encouragement and ran everywhere he went: to the store, to church, to school, and back home again. Soon he was winning community-wide races. In time, as a young man, he sat down and penned this letter to his now-ageing sponsor: 'Guess what now! I run faster than almost anyone in, not only my community, but in all of Kenya. In fact, I have made the Olympic team!'

With tears glistening in her bespectacled eyes, she bowed her head and breathed a prayer for her young Kenyan friend. The year was 1988, and the Olympics would soon be held in Seoul, South Korea. She watched the news reports eagerly.

The day came for his long-distance race. She sat glued to her television set back in Britain, watching for her young man. And when the exhausted racers crossed the finish line, she wept as he captured the silver medal. Her sponsored child, who originally had felt he could do nothing, had grown up to impress the entire world.

Soon news came that the young man's route back home after the Olympic Games would include a plane change in London. He couldn't go home, he said, without first seeing this dear lady. When the day came, this lanky Olympian had to stoop to get through her cottage doorway. There before him, in a wheelchair, sat his champion.

He stood for a moment with tears filling his eyes. Then the handsome young man held out his Olympic medal by its ribbon. 'This is for you,' he finally managed to whisper.

'Oh, no, no, no,' she exclaimed. 'I got to watch you run this time on television. You were right all along. You were so fast! I am so proud of you. I am so very proud of you!'

'No, stop,' he gently interrupted her. 'If you hadn't believed in me when I was eight years old, if you hadn't told that little boy to run, I never would have accomplished this. This is your medal. This is your victory.'

I wish I could promise every person who cares about a child in poverty that an Olympic medal awaits. Not every young boy or girl is genetically put together by the Creator with that ability. But I am absolutely convinced that each and every child is lovingly knit in the mother's womb with the gifts, talents, and potential to accomplish great things – if only given a chance.

Every child matters to God. Once that child, through our intervention, comes to understand and believe the awesome truth, the cold fingers of poverty are pried loose once and for all.

Wess Stafford

www.compassion.com

Eddie Lyle

REPRESENTING **THE VISIONARY** JESUS

I know the plans I have for you . . .
plans to give you hope and a future.

Jeremiah 29:11, NIV

**Eddie Lyle is the Chief Executive of Open Doors, an organization
which exists to serve persecuted Christians. Along with Saltmine,
they are pioneering the Hope Academy during Pentecost 08.
Everybody needs hope to inspire them to a future – both these
organizations are bringing hope by representing the visionary
Jesus.**

In the UK we use millions of tablets to fight depression every year. We have a high rate of teenage suicide. These facts do not seem to suggest a society that is full of hope. Rather, they highlight a society struggling with the reality of the present and despairing at the future.

I've always been struck with a chapter in the Bible – Hebrews 11. It gives a list of people often described as 'heroes of faith'. And it starts with this verse: 'Now faith is being sure of what we hope for and certain of what we do not see.' Then it goes on to describe how these people of faith met the most terrible ends:

> *Some faced jeers and flogging, while still others were chained and put in prison. They were stoned; they were sawn in two; they were put to death by the sword. They went about in sheepskins and goatskins, destitute, persecuted and ill-treated – the world was not worthy of them. They wandered in deserts and mountains, and in caves and holes in the ground. These were all commended for their faith, yet none of them received what had been promised.*
> Hebrews 11:36–39, NIV

They trusted God and were tortured for their faith. God did not give them a magic wand to escape their trouble – and yet they retained their hope. It's amazing, isn't it? But even more amazing is that this is still happening today – there are people who have lost everything because of their determination to serve Jesus, but who have never lost their hope. They are heroes, ordinary Christians living under persecution. It has been my privilege to meet them – and tell their story when I travel home.

Indonesia

Rebekka, Eti and Ratna are three of the loveliest women you could hope to meet. But they were put in prison for three years. Their crime? Telling children about Jesus. At their trial a crowd of Islamic extremists gathered, demanding that they be executed.

When I visited them two years later in Indramayu prison in Indonesia, we entered without any formalities. The guard smiled, nodded his head and let us walk through. Immediately I noticed a bright blue tarpaulin, stretched between the prison bars and the side of a building to form a make-shift church. Underneath was the congregation of Camp David Church, formed by Rebekka. Every Sunday they travel for one and a half hours in a hired minibus to reach the prison so they can worship together.

As I glanced over the congregation, my eyes rested on Ratna and her husband, sitting on the floor. Sadly, their two little children were far away with Ratna's sister's family in Sumatra. Even though she looked very happy, singing loudly and clapping her hands, Ratna told me that she missed them terribly. The last time she had seen them was seven months earlier when they visited during their school break.

That morning I had the privilege of preaching for that congregation. I talked about 'God with us', the story revealed throughout the Bible of a God who does not abandon his people and who goes to tremendous lengths to have a relationship with us. The tangible peace of God in the lives of those three imprisoned mothers powerfully indicated the hope they had found in and through that relationship.

I asked Ratna if she felt that teaching Sunday school classes was worth being imprisoned for; she replied, 'This is nothing compared with the suffering and persecution faced by others. Compared with the Lord's love and what he has given me, it is worth it.'

I produced a bundle of cards for the ladies, from Open Doors supporters in the UK and Ireland. Eti told me, 'So precious are these letters that I cut out the stamps and the senders' names and countries where they live, and I collect them by gluing them into a book. I believe it is a record of my life and it is something I'll never forget.'

When we walked out of that prison, Jesus stayed. I had asked Rebekka whether she had been scared during the court trials. 'I was told that a mob of 200 radical Muslims would be at our first trial. I asked Jesus that morning, "Lord, are you here with us?" "Yes, I am," he replied.'

The presence of Jesus in the darkest moments of our lives – what a difference he makes! 'God with us' is a reality, a promise fulfilled.

Ethiopia

Tulu was the fifth child of eight, but his childhood was marked by an unidentified disease that made him physically weak and a slow learner, which meant he received no education. But as a teenager he became a Christian and experienced God's healing, to the extent that he was able to attend secondary school. He lived in a predominantly Muslim area in southern Ethiopia.

Tulu was deeply touched by God's love. He spent time in prayer and studying the Word of God, and became known for his warmth and affection when sharing God's love with the community. Some Muslim extremists did not appreciate the drastic change in Tulu's life, however, and attacked him with a spear. Even though the spear penetrated his skull, he miraculously recovered after intensive treatment.

'During this time,' his mother recalls, 'there were only four believers in our area, but through Tulu's persecution, fifty people came to know God, including his father and me.'

In the early hours of 2 February 2005, Tulu had excitedly gathered church members to listen to a message from a visiting evangelist before leaving for school. But Ahmed was also on his way to school, carrying his machete. As classes ended, Ahmed confronted Tulu and killed him.

After his arrest, two leaders of Tulu's church visited the local prison and approached Ahmed with a few words of encouragement. Ahmed didn't want to know, but the leaders continued to gently demonstrate God's unconditional love.

Tulu's pastor explained: 'It is through love and prayer that we are able to win our enemies for Christ. That is also why we decided to approach Ahmed and his family with God's love. The Holy Spirit worked in Ahmed – God opened the door, and now we are helping to bring about reconciliation between the two families.'

Their patience in sharing the Gospel and their reassurance that they held no grudge against him helped God's love to break through – and Ahmed accepted Christ as his personal Saviour.

His visitors continued to help him grow in his faith while he was in prison, along with three other believers from a Muslim background. A little more than two years after the murder, Ahmed was baptized in the name of the God he had persecuted. The prison authorities escorted him and the other three prisoners to the church compound and witnessed their baptism ceremony.

The excited new Christians were asked to give their testimonies before being immersed in the water. Ahmed made sure all the witnesses understood that he was being baptized in the name of the Almighty God because of what Jesus had done for him.

The Church in southern Ethiopia suffers intense persecution, but they were willing and able to love and forgive, even a man who had murdered their friend. The Gospel is a message of hope because it changes attitudes and changes people's lives. The dark cloud of murder had the silver lining of forgiveness.

Colombia

Colombia is the fourth largest country in South America, with significant natural resources of oil, gold, silver, emeralds, platinum and coal. Its varied culture reflects the indigenous Indian, Spanish and African origins of its 45 million people. It is also home to illegal armed groups, drug cartels and gross abuses of human rights.

Civil war has raged there for over fifty years. The government has been faced by left-wing rebels and right-wing paramilitary groups. But many believe that the money to be made from drugs and kidnapping is now far more important than any ideological considerations. The same applies to the illegal right-wing paramilitary groups, often backed by drug cartels and landowners, and linked with elements in the army and the police.

Pastors are often targeted by these groups. They are an important influence in local communities, often refusing to be coerced by force, and speaking out against violence and corruption. Many members of the armed groups have turned to Christ and abandoned their former allegiance. Others, sadly, have turned to crime as their armed groups have demobilized – often adding further pressure on local churches and their leaders.

Pastors have been threatened and churches closed. But many have stood the test. In many places churches meet in secret and Christians share their faith, even at the risk of losing their homes – or even their lives.

'We are going to kill you,' the ten guerrilla fighters told Pastor Gabriel, half apologetically. 'Please understand, it's not our decision. We have orders from the high command to kill any pastors who enter our territory.'

Gabriel had been conducting a wedding and baptism service for a new local congregation – the result of his sharing his faith in this area, which was located four hours from his home. This was the fifth time that armed men had abducted him in the seventeen years since he and his wife had moved from Bogotá to pastor a church in Colombia's troubled jungle region.

It was a church that was responding to the needs of the local community – particularly the children orphaned as a result of the war. There were daily hot meals, a playground, and an afternoon drop-in centre where volunteer tutors helped them with their school work.

The previous abductions had ended peaceably, with Gabriel insisting that he was doing God's work and would not take sides or become dependent on co-operation with either the government or the insurgents. So now he asked, 'What have I done to deserve death?'

'First, you talk on the radio about loving your neighbour and living in peace,' they answered. 'Because of you, we think a lot of young people are refusing to join the armed struggle.'

'I preach the Gospel of Jesus Christ,' Gabriel replied. 'God has called me to share Jesus with every Colombian. If preaching the Gospel makes me your enemy – well, that is not my intention. But I cannot disobey God.'

The guerrillas eventually stopped interrogating Gabriel and went away, leaving him alone in the darkness. Gabriel assumed they were planning his execution.

'God, I did not expect to die just now; I haven't finished my work on earth,' he prayed. 'But if it is to be, I ask you two things. Please, raise up another to carry on in my place. Don't let my work be in vain. Second, as you did with Saul of Tarsus when your servant Stephen was martyred, I pray that somebody standing by at my death will turn their life around and come to know you as Lord.'

Gabriel sat alone praying until one o'clock in the morning, when the guerrillas returned. To his surprise, they started to untie the ropes that bound him. 'We are going to give you another opportunity to live,' they said solemnly. 'But, you cannot ever come here again. If you do, we will kill you. We have our orders.'

'Why are you sparing my life?' Gabriel asked.

'Because of those children, those war orphans you help,' they answered. 'Some of them are our orphans. Their parents were our comrades. You're the only one we know who really cares about those children. If we kill you, they will have nobody.'

Jose was 47, the father of 7 children, and for 15 years he had been the pastor of a church with around 400 members. He was also responsible for a school for 150 poor children, and had established a sponsorship programme which supported 200 needy young people.

Last year he was linked to an Open Doors Bible distribution programme which had angered the local rebel militia – they blamed it for the desertion of a large number of guerrillas from their ranks. That was how Jose found himself on a hit list: one of six Christian ministers threatened with death, accused of brainwashing local people.

Then the threats became a reality. Pastor Jose was walking to his home when he was shot five times – and died instantly. At his funeral 4,000 mourners made a peaceful demonstration against violence. Afterwards the remaining pastors met with the police.

The children of church leaders are enormously vulnerable, and their experience of persecution and suffering can easily go unnoticed. In Colombia, Open Doors is bringing hope to many who have lost a parent in the violence, or have been forced to leave their homes.

'Some of these children have been tremendously marked by despair, fear, depression, lack of self-esteem and self-worth. To show them the love of Christ, to fulfil a need and accompany that with prayer and some strategic follow-up, can make a life-changing difference in the hearts of the children as well as the parents,' says the Regional Director of Open Doors Latin America.

Hope at Christmas

That's why last year we made sure these children had something to celebrate when Christmas came round. Supporters generously sent in donations to provide Christmas dinners, Christmas presents – and the opportunity to start school for the first time.

We were deeply touched when we received the news of how the children had responded. One young pastor's wife had promised her son and daughter a present this time, but as Christmas Day approached she realized with great sadness that once again she could not afford to keep her promise. But now there were presents. As she watched her children open their bags and pull out new toys and clothes, she said, 'This truly is God's provision!'

Just one week before a pastor had received a death-threat, and was given three days to leave town. Yet he and his wife took the time to bring their family to the Christmas celebration. With tears in their eyes, they said, 'The Lord takes care of us and gives us exactly what we need!'

Your response

Open Doors began way back in the 1950s. God called a young Dutchman named Andrew to respond to a verse in the Bible (Rev. 3:2, NIV): 'Wake up! Strengthen what remains and is about to die.' It prompted him to go to Poland – which was then behind the Iron Curtain, in the grip of Soviet Russian communism.

He found a forgotten church, their voice unheard by the rest of the world. They were desperate for Bibles – so Brother Andrew became 'God's Smuggler', taking car-load after car-load of Bibles across borders, constantly praying that the guards would not see the Bibles.

Now Brother Andrew is fifty years older – but still full of the passion for the good news about Jesus, and for helping people to discover him for themselves – still passionate about getting Christians who have freedom to worship to remember the members of the Christian family who do not have that freedom.

He often refers to his first trip to the Eastern Bloc, back in July 1955, when he spoke on the platform of a Baptist church in Warsaw. The pastor said to him at the end of the service: 'Young man, your words today are not the important thing. It's you – being here.'

From that moment on he knew what he was called to do – it was simply to be there.

Jesus said (in Matthew 25:35–40, NIV):

For I was hungry and you gave me something to eat, I was thirsty and you gave me something to drink, I was a stranger and you invited me in, I needed clothes and you clothed me, I was sick and you looked after me, I was in prison and you came to visit me. . . whatever you did for one of the least of these brothers of mine, you did for me.

Brother Andrew discovered that his presence brought hope and encouragement to persecuted Christians. But that was because he had already discovered that God's presence brings hope – hope by changing lives, hope by giving courage to face the present and the future, hope in giving purpose to life, setting out on the great adventure of faith.

Pentecost saw the coming of God's presence by his Holy Spirit. Across the world God is still present by his Holy Spirit – strengthening, encouraging, comforting, bringing hope. He still calls us to stand alongside the helpless, and to bring them hope by being there for them and pointing them to the One who provides us all with a sure hope. How will you bring that hope to those you are called alongside?

Eddie Lyle
www.opendoorsuk.org
www.saltmine.org

REPRESENTING
THE PEACEMAKING
JESUS

Blessed are the peacemakers, for they will be called sons of God.

Matthew 5:9, NIV

Wizdom is a member of GreenJade, a Christian hip-hop group signed to Survivor Records. In partnership with Survivor and the schools charity XLP, they have been running the GunzDown tour, encouraging inner-city schoolchildren to lay down their guns and knives. By doing this they represent the peacemaking Jesus.

As a member of the 'Tru skool' Hip-Hop group GreenJade, I am privileged to be called to a ministry that is somewhat out of the ordinary. We spent five years pioneering Holy Hip-Hop in the black churches in the UK, helping it to arrive at a place where Grime, Hip Hop and R'n'B acts have superseded the traditional appeal of Gospel choirs. We spent the following five years performing in the charismatic white churches, where we were one of the first 'Urban' groups in recent memory to consistently perform at premier events such as Spring Harvest, Greenbelt, Soul Survivor, SPACE and New Wine. Unfortunately there is a divide between the black and white churches in the UK, but we were able to play a part in opening the doors for the likes of 29th Chapter, 4 Kornerz and Jahaziel to cross over after the retirement of the World Wide Message Tribe.

Since we began in 1996, our goal has always been to return with a message of hope to people who were searching for some meaning to life, just like we had been. We aim to show them the answers we had found and demonstrate Christ's relevance to our individual everyday lives, in the world in which we live.

In 1995, about 14 members of the then 25-strong 'Green Jade Sect', as we were then known (no religious connotations – the name came from a Kung-Fu film!), committed their lives to Christ's rule! We had seen for ourselves Christ's power to change lives when a 'beef' (disagreement) involving one of our members that was spiralling out of control (and was beginning to take the rest of us with it) was miraculously brought to a conclusion (or 'squashed'). A woman at a friend's work-place had seen him distracted and distressed, so invited him to pray with her during their lunch-break. He had tried everything else by this point and had taken to carrying a Samurai sword around with him for 'protection'. At this time he also purchased his first firearm, so he figured that praying couldn't hurt!

A few weeks later he decided he would give his life to Christ's rule, and the very same evening he unexpectedly bumped into the guy who had put a contract out on his life. The guy who had ordered the hit head-butted our member – a blow that resulted in stitches. But instead of reacting and fighting back, mindful of his decision to change his life, our friend replied, 'Okay, it's over now!' and turned his back. It was over! Coming from a place where our guy had at one point been chased through south-west London by a group of guys wielding weapons, looking to kill him, the fact that one blow had ended the whole feud was quite miraculous!

He decided he would investigate 'this Jesus thing' further and encouraged the other members to do the same, even inviting his new pastor down to one of our legendary 'Hip-Hop, weed & Kung Fu' Friday nights at Wei's flat in Clapham. Slowly we all went to check it out for ourselves. Although not all of the fourteen who gave their lives to Christ's rule stayed committed to the faith, the remnant – namely: Judah, Wei, 3rd Son, Wizdom (all of GreenJade); Holy Hip-Hop artist Jahaziel; Minister David Skyers, Matthew, and a few others – have all continued to be a positive influence to their immediate and extended communities.

Our prayer is that everyone exposed to GreenJade, whether Christian or not, is able to see a positive example of young, mainly black men trying to live their lives as directed by Christ, and having a positive effect on society at large!

On Old Year's Night of 2002, GreenJade were performing at a New Year's 'Celebration' in Birmingham in front of what could only be described as a truly miserable Christian crowd at the Bethel Convention Centre. After we had finished our set and could hang around no longer, we started our drive back down the M40, amazed that Christians who are supposed to be living an abundant, blessed life could respond in such a lacklustre way to the fact that they had made it into a new year! As we talked and argued (GreenJade is practically a family, so most conversations between us are impassioned), we started hearing reports on the radio of a shooting in Birmingham in which two girls had lost their lives. Those two girls turned out to be Charlene Ellis and Latisha Shakespear, 18 and 17, who were gunned down, innocent victims of a gang feud that family members had been caught in.

These events impassioned our conversation all the more. Here we were, coming back from an event with a miserable crowd to whom abundant and joyous life had been made available, while a few miles down the road two teenage girls lost their lives while trying to have a fun night out. We decided on two things that night:

1. There must be some sort of response from the Body of Christ with regard to the rise in violence amongst our young people; and
2. We would continue to actively live out God's Word through *agape* (active, unconditional, selfless, Godly love) in our actions and behaviour towards others.

To an extent, all of the group members are engaged with young people and/or our community! 3rd Son is a Finance Officer for Lewisham Council. Wei works with young adults with learning difficulties and mental illness. Judah is an Education Welfare Officer for Southwark Council and runs parenting workshop classes. Secret coaches basketball at a college in Havering. And I (Wizdom) have worked for the probation service and in a drug rehabilitation centre. However, through our music, inspired by our faith, we wanted to make a larger statement about the fact that God has something to say about gun and knife crime.

We wrote the song 'Gunz Down' and started to perform it. I told a boy I mentor, who was 16 at the time, that we had this song and wanted it to make a difference to what was happening 'on road' with regard to kids with guns. He was very polite and said that what we wanted to do was good, but did we 'really think making another song would actually make a difference?' I started to defend my point, but then stopped and listened to what he had just said. It was as if the lights came on. We didn't need another catchy song telling people guns are bad. We needed to meet with people picking up guns at their point of need and challenge them with an alternative way of resolving conflict!

We realized that to be effective, we could not start with the people already holding weapons but with the kids who were at risk of picking them up, and we had to find a safe environment to engage with them. Schools were the obvious place to try and engage the youth, and we were about to encounter a situation that would make this all the more poignant.

On 9 July 2005, ZionNoiz (the Hip-Hop crew to which we are affiliated) were scheduled to perform at an anti-gun-crime youth event in a church hall in Clapham, which youth from the area would be attending. We came on and were a few songs into our set and about to perform 'Gunz Down' when a scuffle broke out in the crowd. Security moved in and separated the two groups of youths, ejecting one group while the other was locked inside. It turned out that one member of the group left inside had a knife and was trying to force his way out to finish the fight. Security managed to regain control of the situation as we stood on stage watching.

We finally got everything calmed down and were about to restart the performance when we heard a bang, and two masked men (or rather, boys) ran into the hall. One of them was carrying a huge silver hand-gun. (It was so big, it reminded us of the 'Megatron Transformer' toy guns they used to make when we were kids!) They told everyone to get on the floor, but by this time it was pandemonium, with kids running for their lives and screaming! I looked down to the right side of the stage and saw a large group of kids, some as young as eight years old, packed on top of each other, desperately trying to hide behind one of the stage speakers.

As we were still standing up, mainly in shock and elevated on the stage, the gunman walked up to us and scanned his pistol across us, stopping at 3rd and pointing it in his chest! They then fled the scene, having proved the point that they had the power.

Different members reacted differently to this event, but I was furious! I had to drive to my sister's home in Hertfordshire that same night, and I realized whilst on the M25 that for a whole hour I had been arguing with myself about what I should have done in that situation. I pulled the car over to the hard shoulder and prayed that God would calm me down, as all I could think of was how I could hurt the people who had put me in that position of fear. I realized this was unproductive and was exactly the rage felt by people who had been held up at gun/knife-point, and who then got 'tooled up' themselves for revenge. I, however, had God to pray to and was mature enough to know that revenge would be stupid and would just add to the cycle of violence. But most kids don't have the same maturity or Christian understanding that I had. So we had to help them.

This experience made us all the more determined to do something. We sat down with Patrick Regan of the schools charity XLP and discussed the possibility of doing an anti-guns schools tour. He was really interested in the idea, as he had just returned from doing gang mediation in Trench Town, Jamaica, which sees 1,400 murders a year in a country whose population is only 2.7 million (compared to London's 200 or so annual murders within a population of 7 million). We agreed that we needed to do something pre-emptive, as we were concerned that once young people get involved in guns and gang activity, it is incredibly difficult to get them out of it.

We had an animated video created in conjunction with Undercurrent Comics' Sam119 character. Sulé Bryan and Richard Poet created the ground-breaking music video for us and blessed us, telling us the only payment they wanted was the message getting out there! We took some time off work (as we couldn't find any funding to go full time), pulled in some favours for the sound equipment, and went into the schools.

After the first pilot show the headmaster came on stage to say that he had been a youth worker in a youth club some years previously, and one night a boy came into the club with a knife and was messing around with it. One of the boy's friends had taken the knife from him and was holding it to his neck as a joke. Suddenly someone accidentally pushed the boy with the knife, which plunged into the neck of the boy who had brought it in. The boy died in the arms of the now headteacher. He had never forgotten the waste of life he had witnessed that night.

After another show a boy was brought to me (who I shall refer to as 'Steve'). Although slightly reluctant, he said, 'I enjoyed the show, especially the part about if you retaliate, things get worse. The only thing is, I think that message is a bit late for me!' I asked him why and Steve went on to explain that his cousin had been shot and killed, and he, his older brother and some friends had gone out for revenge. This resulted in his elder brother being shot and stabbed but surviving, and his best friend being shot to death.

Steve said that where he lived, you had to be part of a gang to be safe. To go through certain areas, you had to print off a 'passport' from a website – otherwise you would be 'taxed'! He also said that he wanted to get out of the gang but couldn't, because his brother was involved and it wasn't something you could just leave. What I found all the more alarming was that he was only 15 and had taken to wearing a bullet-proof vest to school for protection.

Along with XLP, his school's pastoral leader and Les Isaac of the Ascension Trust (a part of Street Pastors), we were able to provide support and mentoring for the boy, and we even went to his home and prayed with his family. Unfortunately his fears for his life were realized six weeks after the tour, when he survived being stabbed in the neck by an older boy in his school who was part of a rival gang. While we continued to work with him, it was felt that the safest thing for his life was to send him back to Jamaica (away from Trench Town) to stay with his father. He is there now and, thankfully, all reports are that he is doing well.

At 15 Steve was slightly older than our core audience. This underlines the need to catch kids before they turn 14 or 15, because by then they may have already begun on the paths that can ultimately lead to gun/knife crime. This is evident in every inner-city school where we have performed to pupils in Year 9 and above! This doesn't detract from the need to reach those who are already active in gun/knife crime, but we needed to find an appropriate way of pitching the tour.

Since starting the tour in 2005, we have plainly seen that fear, low self-worth, ignorance and the absence of fathers (now referred to as 'Dadlessness') are the main drivers behind youth violence. Over the past two decades the removal of parental rights and moral standards, coupled with the effect of family breakdown, have propelled the rise in disenfranchised youth. The Christian faith and moral code have been all but abolished in mainstream schools and replaced with individual human rights. Unfortunately, a human's right to act selfishly and disregard the needs/lives of others is the foundation that supports our materialistic, binge-drinking, antisocial, amoral, secular society in which prematurely sexualized youth have given birth to children while yet children themselves, and are thus unequipped to sufficiently empower their kids.

I remember a conversation with one of the clients in the residential drug rehab I worked in, who said to me that it wasn't until he was 21 that he realized that there was anything wrong with breaking the law. All of his family used drugs and most had been to jail, so for him that was 'normal'. It is this mind-set of normalcy that needs to be challenged, and I believe this is where the Body of Christ can help.

A few months back I decided I wanted to read the Gospels of Jesus again, and I realized something that I hadn't really noticed before. Jesus did not start preaching until he had finished healing! Jesus' first question to many was, 'What can I do for you?' He talked with the Samaritan woman at the well about the issues in her life before he revealed who he really was – the Messiah! He healed the sick and diseased before he preached the Sermon on the Mount. In other words, Jesus took practical social action before he began to convert anyone. The general public is often dubious of the Christian faith because of past damage caused by the 'Christian Religion' and its administration by certain denominations of Christianity, but I believe that part of our mandate is to engage with the world and simply ask the question, 'How can we help you?' We have found that when young people respect your talent, they will listen to whatever it is you have to say, so we continue to use our musical gifts as an ice-breaker to who we are and what we represent. If we help people out and represent God with compassion, care, excellence and due diligence, then when the Holy Spirit calls them, they will be in a position to receive him.

Gun and knife violence is not a black-on-black problem; it is often a 'poor-on-poor' problem in deprived inner-city areas. England has the lowest social mobility rate (the ability to move from one social class to another) of all the developed countries (i.e. Europe and America), and life at the lower end of the scale is such a battle that the mind-set of having to fight for every little crumb often finds its way onto the streets! This is coupled with a large immigrant population who have come from a background of war in their recent past, which has made violence more acceptable within their behaviour. Somalis, Yugoslavs and Sierra Leonians have all come to the UK from areas that have seen real violence in their recent history, and when faced with violence here, they often react in a way that may appear out of proportion, but which is fuelled by the things they have seen. This is evident in areas such as Woolwich in south-east London, where there have been numerous reports of gang violence involving young members of the immigrant communities.

While we are not in the position to put to rights all of life's ills, our aim is to do our part in creating a community of positive musical influence that provides an option for the listeners. For this precise reason our current album is called *LIFE As We Know It*, to show that there is another way, and that we all have the power to change our lives! We all have our part to play for the good of our kids. What is yours?

Wizdom

www.GreenJade.co.uk
www.GunzDown.com
www.XLP.org.uk
www.survivor.co.uk

Shell Perris

REPRESENTING
THE CREATIVE
JESUS

God saw all that he had made, and it was very good.

Genesis 1:31, NIV

Shell Perris is a writer and musician signed to Authentic Media. She believes that Jesus is the greatest creator who has ever lived, and that the greatest place to find the best in creativity should be in the Church. Through their work, Authentic are representing the creative Jesus.

Over the years, music has proved to be a fantastic way of communicating to people of all ages across the globe. Whether you're into pop, rock, rap, hip-hop, heavy metal, soul, R&B, jazz, swing, classical, country or a bit of legendary punk, music seems to be a way forward for everyone. It's a common denominator; a conversation starter; a topic guaranteed to create a response not only in the mind but also in the heart. Why? Because everyone has a favourite song, or a song that sparks a memory, or a song that makes them feel a certain way, or a song that marks an era. I'm guessing that even now, as you're reading these words, meaningful songs that have played a part in your life so far are popping into your head and reminding you of past times! It's like when my mum and dad are at a disco and a song from the seventies starts playing, and every time, guaranteed, one of them will say, 'This is what we used to dance to when we were your age!' Then they return to bouncing around on the dance floor because it seems that they didn't know how to dance when they were my age either!

You only have to look at the world around you and the people in it to see how music and creativity play a part in our lives. I have spent the last five years of my life working with young people, and I have seen just how much music affects them and their world. Teenagers' bedrooms say it all! It starts off when they find a favourite band. Then they buy the albums, the posters, the ring-tones, the concert tickets, the DVDs, the T-shirts . . . the list goes on and on. When it's great music with great lyrics performed by great role models, it's all well and good. However, so much of the music that young people listen to today talks about doing whatever it takes to make yourself feel good. Do we really want to sit back and watch this generation slip into thinking that it's perfectly acceptable to take drugs, sleep around, get drunk, self-harm, and so on, because a song or a band or an artist implies that it's okay? No! It's almost as if some celebrities are more famous for going into rehab to fight an addiction or being sent to prison, than for what they actually started off being famous for. Why? Because that's what sells newspapers and magazines.

I distinctly remember a particular trip to the supermarket just over a year ago. I was walking over to the front of the shop to collect a trolley and I noticed a little girl, in a white dress, sitting on a small moving ride. As she was being gently swayed from one side to the other she was singing a song called *Because of You* by Kelly Clarkson. Her cute child's voice sounded beautiful as she sang at the top of her voice, but she was too young to stop and think about the words she was singing. I saw in the way she was smiling and enjoying herself that she was totally unaware of the picture that was being painted by the song's lyrics. She was actually singing about a young woman who'd had an unhappy childhood and blamed someone significant in her life for her pain. But to the little girl on the ride it was just a song she'd heard on the radio and seen on TV … more of a lullaby than a song that told a painful story.

Another thing happened a few months ago. Tim (my hubby) and I were sat with our friends in a coffee lounge at Liverpool airport. Our flight had been delayed and so we were just chilling out and chatting away. Tim and Dan went off to sort out the hire-car situation, and Claire and I drank some more tea. To the right of us there were some mechanical massage chairs. Three children accompanied by two women ran over to the chairs and sat on them. One of the children, a girl 7 or 8 years old, knelt on the floor in between the two massage chairs. All of a sudden she began to sing and dance in an extremely sexual way. I was astonished and shocked that a girl of her age knew how to be so perverse. As Steve Mawston says in his book, *Who Do You Think You Are?*, we are constantly bombarded with messages from the media. So where do we, the Church of Jesus Christ, go from here?

As I have travelled around over the last few years, performing and working with people from a variety of ages, churches and backgrounds, I have been encouraged by what I have seen – creativity within the Church!

I have seen theatres, parks, show-grounds, schools, churches, nightclubs, holiday camps, stadiums and city centres full of people worshipping God. I have witnessed thousands of lost people being found and welcomed into God's kingdom. I have met fired-up Christians who have scarcely been able to stop and breathe, so great is the excitement that God has put within them to spread the word.

I used to work for an organization called Innervation Trust (the creators of 'thebandwithnoname', 'tbc' and the network of 'Collective' schools bands). They are dedicated to presenting the Christian message to young people through music. They understand the power of creativity and are on the front line when it comes to using a combination of music, dance and God's Word to see this generation won for Jesus. This is what Chip K from thebandwithnoname had to say about it all:

A while ago, thebandwithnoname did a gig at York Minster. . . . I'll never forget the immensity of that ancient church. Our music seemed to reverberate for an eternity as the track echoed past the stained-glass windows and up into those gothic high ceilings. Quite a sound! The very next day we did an outdoor concert in Birmingham. Just like the York Minster gig, this one was attended by hundreds of young Christians, all of them praising and worshipping God with us. Only this time, instead of being cooped up inside an ancient church, we were right out on the streets, just outside what looked like the town hall or something downtown. As I gazed at the crowd among the urban high-rise buildings, I couldn't help but think that actually this was a better representation of what the early Church must've been like and indeed, what Church today should look like. A massive group of people enjoying God right out in the open air, while unbelievers and passers-by stared at them, wondering what in the world was going on.

You see, people are always looking for something different – something that stands out from everyday normality. When they see a poster stuck up outside a church that advertises a pop/rock concert, they think, 'That's different. Let's go and check it out.' When they walk through the town centre and see a bunch of Christians being creative and excellent, they stop and watch what's going on. When they see young people picking up litter and participating in community projects, it's noticed, and it creates some kind of response within them. Our job is to make sure that the response is a positive one and not a negative one – a response that draws them closer and doesn't push them away.

The Church of Jesus Christ is not lacking in people with creative talents and abilities. I am constantly amazed at the number of people I meet within the Church who are dancers or singers or artists or musicians or actors or creative leaders or people who simply love being creative. There are Christians all over the place with massive dreams, big visions and vast amounts of passion and determination, who desperately want to see the Holy Spirit at work in the lives of the people they come into contact with. Look at the hundreds, if not thousands, of Christian organizations out there whose sole purpose is to tell people about God. Have you ever stepped inside a Christian book/music store? If you have, you will have seen shelves displaying thousands of products that have all been inspired by God. A vast array of music, books, poetry, films, readings, pieces of art – all done by creative people from around the world who love God and want to make him known. Honestly – it's crazy! God has blessed many people with a gift of creativity, and recognizing that as soon as possible is a great thing.

I believe the next thing we need to do is to ask the right questions: What can we do to create a positive response within the local community and, indeed, the world? How can we use creativity to influence the lives of people around us? How can we be culturally relevant and prophetically relevant at the same time? Wow – that's a big question! Let me say it again: How can we be culturally relevant and prophetically relevant at the same time?

I believe that being culturally relevant means being creative in our thinking and using our eyes to see what's going on around us. Being prophetically relevant means being even more creative in our thinking and using our hearts to sense what God is doing around us! It's about being one step ahead; it's about thinking outside of the box; it's about laying aside our own plans, thoughts and agendas and allowing God to do what he's extremely good at – being creative! We serve an unbelievably creative God – he's a designer. You only have to look at the world and the people around us to work that one out. He is the ultimate Creator of creativity! Look at the Bible. Creativity is mentioned in so many different places: the playing of musical instruments; people dancing and singing and acting; the creative reading of God's Word. Jesus himself was the most famous storyteller around! He was different and original, and that's why such large crowds of people were drawn to him.

I don't know about you, but I do not want to be copying other people's ideas and always being one step behind. I want to show initiative – I want to be a trend-setter! I want to lead the way so that other people will follow. I want to hear God's voice and go where he is telling me to go. Can you imagine what it would be like if we, as a united Church, could get into that way of thinking?! I realize that's not everyone's cup of tea, but what does the Bible say?

> *I didn't take on their way of life. I kept my bearings in Christ – but I entered their world and tried to experience things from their point of view. I've become just about every sort of servant there is in my attempts to lead those I meet into a God-saved life. I did all this because of the Message. I didn't just want to talk about it; I wanted to be in on it!*
>
> 1 Corinthians 9:21–24, The Message Bible

It's so exciting to see that more and more Christians are waking up to the fact that God is on the move. 'Things aren't like they used to be a hundred years ago. It's not even like it used to be twenty years ago.' I remember going through a stage when all I seemed to hear people say in response to those statements was, 'And the sooner the Church realizes that, the better.' Well, do you know what? I believe the Church *is* realizing that! I believe in the Church.

So, I think we may have established that the Church, as a whole, is full of creativity and that we need to be asking the right sort of questions. The last ingredient I think we need is a massive dose of boldness! We need to be creative dreamers, prophetic thinkers and bold warriors – there's a mission statement if ever I've heard one! We have got to be prepared to step outside our comfort zones and know that it's not going to be easy, it's not going to be comfortable, and it's going to take every bit of energy that we have. But again, what does the Bible say?

> *Those who sow in tears will reap with songs of joy.*
> Psalm 126:5, NIV

For me, this poem by an anonymous author says it all:

> *Today I prayed,*
> *Disturb me, Lord, when my dreams come true,*
> *Only because I have dreamed too small.*
> *Disturb me when I arrive safely,*
> *Only because I sailed too close to the shore.*
> *Disturb me when things I have gained,*
> *Cause me to lose my thirst for more of you.*
> *Disturb me when I have acquired success,*
> *Only to lose my desire for excellence.*
> *Disturb me when I give up too soon,*
> *And settle too far short of the goals you have set for my life.*
> Based on Colossians 3:1–2

So if you're serious about living this new resurrection life with Christ, act like it. Pursue the things over which Christ presides. Don't shuffle along, eyes to the ground, absorbed with the things right in front of you. Look up, and be alert to what is going on around Christ – that's where the action is. See things from his perspective.

Colossians 3:1–2, The Message Bible

When we link creativity, prophetic thinking and boldness together and look at the world through eyes that have eternal perspective . . . that's when we see God do unimaginable things. That's when heavenly fingerprints are left on the hearts and lives of the people we meet. That's when we stop and God is given permission to start.

I will finish with one final thought. Six months after becoming a Christian, I went to a church event in Warrington, Cheshire, where a guy called Dave Tierney was speaking. It was on that night, at that event, that God, through a word of prophecy, gave me a dream and a purpose – to be a healer of broken hearts through my music.

I remember getting home and feeling overwhelmed by God's presence – so much so that I couldn't speak to anyone (which is quite a rarity for me!). I walked into my bedroom, closed the door behind me and just sat on my bed, waiting expectantly for God to speak to me again. I knew I had to read my Bible, so I began to read Isaiah 61. To my amazement, these were the words I read:

The Spirit of God, the Master, is on me
because God anointed me.
He sent me to preach good news to the poor,
heal the heartbroken . . .

Isaiah 61:1, The Message Bible

My eyes grew wide with excitement and I laughed under my breath, barely able to believe it!

At the time I didn't really understand what it all meant; I didn't get what any of it had to do with me. But now, after years of being a 'healer of broken hearts through music', I understand. . . .

God is always on the alert, constantly on the lookout for people who are totally committed to him.

2 Chronicles 16:9, The Message Bible

Don't let anything get in the way of what God is calling you to do. Satan loves to work things and twist things round so that creativity, prophetic thinking and boldness are dampened. Cynicism, religious attitudes, fear, doubt, loss of faith and passion, lack of confidence – they can all create turmoil within us that ultimately leads to us missing God-given opportunities, and overlooking God's will. Hold on tight to the words that God has spoken to you and the promises that he has given to you, and see them through. After all, if we're not going to . . . who is?

Shell Perris
www.authenticmedia.co.uk

Andy Kind

REPRESENTING
THE LAUGHING
JESUS

. . . the joy of the LORD is your strength.

Nehemiah 8:10, NIV

Andy Kind is a professional comedian. He will be performing at the Emerging Culture comedy event as part of Pentecost 08. He is passionate about helping the Church in the serious business of rediscovering the joy of Jesus, and as such he represents the laughing Jesus.

Each one should use whatever gift he or she has received to serve others, faithfully administering God's grace in its various forms.
1 Peter 4:10, NIV

Somebody once came up to me at the end of a gig, looked me straight in the eye and said, 'You're a Christian? But you seem so normal!'

'Sorry, I'll try to fit in less from now on!'

That sort of comment is par for the course when you're a Christian on the national comedy circuit. People – for the most part, anyway – find difficulty in marrying the idea of Christianity with that of the ruthless, pub-based, drug- and sex-dominated world of stand-up comedy.

From certain areas of the Christian community, there is always intrigue at how I find it possible to operate within such an environment, without being repulsed by – and having to cross myself at – the content of some of the shows. Or how I am able to maintain my own integrity, when all the audience wants, at times, is what we term 'lowest-common-denominator jokes'.

For a proportion of non-Christians, the confusion is much more straightforward: 'I didn't realize Christians had a sense of humour!'

But the surprise that is shown, both by members of the Church and by those who spend their Sunday mornings in bed, has without doubt been a contributory factor to me venturing into stand-up comedy in the first place.

Over the last few years, I have become increasingly frustrated by the barriers that exist between the secular and the Christian worlds. It's amazing how Christians can become pigeon-holed as pure stereotypes: bland, lifeless spoilsports who drink only tea and sing 'Kum By Yah', whilst shunning social interaction and passing judgement on anything they see as ungodly – such as fun or loud music. How such a vast community can be compartmentalized by a sweeping generalization of this ilk is beyond me, but people manage it.

Having said that, in many cases it rings worryingly true. I'm not sure that, as Christians, we always do enough to engage with the secular world, to embrace mainstream society and to break down some of the partitions that exist.

What makes us accessible, and what we *think* makes us accessible are two different things. For example, where I live in Stoke, there is this one 'Christian' guy who stands in the centre of town every Tuesday and preaches the Gospel. Sorry, did I say 'preaches'? I meant 'spits'.

His entire *raison d'être*, it would appear, is to spend one day a week telling stress- and shopping-laden passers-by that they are going to hell unless they stop worshipping the devil.

Now, soap-box evangelism of the fire-and-brimstone variety may well have had its converts over the course of history, but bullying a couple of souls into the kingdom does not mean that, as a rule, this style of preaching is not hugely destructive!

The hateful vehemence with which this man in my home-town delivers his sermons is as far away from the spirit of Christ's ministry as it is possible to stray. Purely from a performance and public-speaking aspect, there is absolutely nothing engaging or accessible about standing on a box and loudly spouting vitriolic diatribes. Where is the dialogue? Where is the option for debate? Where on earth is the love?!

For every one person who is brought closer to God by this style of 'evangelism', there are thousands who are pushed further away. This would be obvious if the man in question bothered to make even the slightest hint of eye-contact with any of his audience. Every speaker–listener dialogue is based on trust, and it is impossible to trust someone who is unable to make eye-contact. If this man did look his prospective converts in the eye, he would simply see scorn and distaste reflected back at him. And he might stop. I'm sure he feels he has been given a word from the Lord. As far as I'm concerned, that word should be 'Sshh!!'

Everything we do reflects on Jesus, whether we like it or not. And sadly, the public face of Christianity and the Church often does nothing but push people further away from the Truth. This realization was one of the two main driving forces behind my route into comedy – the other being that I'm completely obsessed with making people laugh! By being active on the circuit and being good at what I do, I hope to be able to show some of the cynics out there that it is possible to have a living, working faith in Christ, while at the same time engaging in a relevant, 'normal' way with mainstream society.

I have always felt, furthermore, that if someone can relate to you on a human level, they are much more likely to relate to you on a spiritual one. And within the context of comedy, someone will only laugh if they can indeed relate to the humour. All laughter is based on recognition.

In late 2005, my friend and fellow comedian, Tony Vino, rang me up and said, 'Andy, we've been given a prophecy – check out Genesis 21, verse 6.' So I did, and this is what it said (NIV):

God has brought me laughter, and everyone who hears about this will laugh with me.

As I'm sure you all know, it refers to the birth of Isaac, when God delivered Sarah and Abraham a son, despite the fact that they were both older than Albert Steptoe. Sarah was 90, though a mere pup compared to Abraham, who was one off a century at 99. What a cradle-snatcher!

For Tony and I, this passage about God bringing laughter was a hugely pertinent and inspiring one, as it was given to us at a time when we had been discussing profoundly our desire to take comedy into churches as a form of evangelism.

I'd been performing on the comedy circuit for almost a year, and had been very quick to nail my Christian colours to the mast. As a result, I'd already witnessed just how intrigued onlookers can become when the concepts of Christianity and comedy converge – to the point where, at almost every gig I did, someone would ask me about my faith (and usually apologize for any swear-words they may have used in my presence!).

We decided to form 'The Isaac Project' (*Isaac* is Hebrew for 'he laughs'). God had spoken, and so we would usher in a new age of cutting-edge comedy evangelism! What followed was a period of busyness, as we bombarded as many Christian publications as we could with details of who we were and what we planned to achieve. Happily, one major magazine took up the story and published a very positive article in their December 2005 issue. And slowly but surely the offers started to roll in, and churches started booking stand-up comedy nights as part of their calendar.

I should say at this stage that The Isaac Project is not the first example of UK comedians taking comedy into churches. John Archer (*Undercover Magic*, Sky One) and Tim Vine (*Not Going Out*, BBC1) are two hugely talented and successful comics who have been touring churches for years, and both have been massively pioneering in blazing a trail for others to follow. But two comedians do not make a culture, and the vision Tony and I have had from the inception of 'Isaac' is of a network – a community, if you like – of Christians using comedy as a form of evangelism throughout the UK – a format to rival and imitate the thriving scene in the US.

Over there in the States, comedy is a much stronger and more central part of the Christian culture. There are far more people involved in the industry who have a working faith in the big JC, and the quality of the performers on the other side of the Atlantic is reassuringly impressive.

The idea of evangelistic comedy is a much less alien concept in the United States, and there are a good number of organizations and performers of note. For a start, there is the Christian Comedy Association (CCA) – 'An association of Christians committed to offering faith-affirming truth through the craft of comedy.' The CCA currently resources and connects over 300 comics across the USA and beyond – now that's a community!

Also of note are the likes of 'Outreach Comedy', an agency that seeks to 'equip the Church with sound guidance and great tools for the makings of effective comedy events', and then 'The Ultimate Comedy Theatre', a company set up by Kenn Kington – a top comedian in his own right – which stages high-profile comedy events around the country.

It would be wonderful to develop something proportional to that network in the UK, and I believe it will happen, because I see that it is already starting to happen. The Church is now starting to use comedy to engage with our post-modern culture.

You may notice that I'm avoiding using the phrase 'Christian comedy'. This is quite intentional. When I think of 'Christian comedy', my mind shoots to images of middle-aged vicars doing jokes about two disciples walking into a bar. . . .

When I describe myself – and I'm sure Vine, Archer and others would agree – I say I'm a comedian who happens to be a Christian. I don't tell jokes which start, 'Hey, you know when you're reading Leviticus . . .' or anything insipid like that. There are those who would class such pseudo-religious humour as 'comedy', but anyone who does should be sent back to the times of Leviticus. . . .

The comedy I want to see in churches is not about silly things that the verger may have said, or slightly risqué gags about the organ. I want to see cutting-edge, observational comedy – comedy that challenges and heals. I want to be part of events that show the joy of faith in all its fullness, but that are not afraid to challenge the overly religious sides of God's Church.

Back to the story. . . .

Tony Vino and I started 'living the dream' with The Isaac Project, prayerfully trying to follow where God led us. Our first gig was in Doncaster in February 2006.

We turned up on the evening full of purpose, convinced that this was our calling and that we would therefore be amazing. After all, when God calls you to something, how can you go wrong?

We were terrible. I mean, really, *really* bad. About 200 people saw us fall flat on our faces, when I'm sure they would rather have been doing something much more enjoyable. . . .

The night itself was not a success, and I'm sure any non-Christians there have not ventured into a church outreach event since. However, ironically we came away from the gig with a great sense of purpose and confidence – a certainty that next time we would do it right. Why? Because we had learned how *not* to do it!

Hebrews 12:5 (NIV) says:

Do not make light of the Lord's discipline, and do not lose heart when he rebukes you. . . .

A comedian is like an inventor; his set is like the invention. The finished product is always the result of a cavalcade of mistakes (a comedy of errors), leading to a successful conclusion. The problem is that, unlike an inventor, when a comedian makes a mistake, hundreds of people are there to witness it!

One would hope that you could pray for something and all would be well. But even when God calls you to something, this does not exclude the possibility of suffering or hard times (for suffering, see Jesus).

We're so set, these days, upon a system of instant gratification. 'I was a good person today; I started a vigilante movement that halved street crime in the Stoke-on-Trent area, I uncovered a secret smuggling ring within the local Methodist Church network, and I helped an old lady across the road. Therefore tomorrow, with any luck, God will make me win the Lottery.'

As it happens, I did none of the above things today – although I'm keeping my eye on the Methodist Church! It's just an example of how we are very demanding when it comes to expecting things from God. What we need to do is to realize that he works in his own time – as annoying as that may be.

What I've learned from doing comedy – and from the night in Doncaster in particular – is that, whenever I have a bad gig, I actually get a little bit better. For me, having somebody not laugh at my jokes is akin to them hacking out my heart with a scimitar – it hurts. But it always makes me think, 'Well, how can I do it differently?' And so, by trial and error, you weed out all the negative or weak or unfunny parts, while trying to write new gags that blossom and bloom. (One thing I'm planning on weeding out immediately is erroneous gardening metaphors!) And that's what God did in Doncaster – he allowed us to get it wrong, thereby allowing us to get it right in the end.

And God's plan for comedy is going from strength to strength! As I write this, The Isaac Project had been invited to hundreds of gigs around the country, and its impact is growing. At one church in outer London, the number of people attending was double that which they would expect on a Sunday morning. In Glasgow, we witnessed two rowdy teenage lads in Celtic shirts give their lives to God at the end of the show. We have seen fellow comedians from the comedy circuit open up to God in dramatic fashion, and there have been a number of reports passed onto us of people coming into a church environment for the first time to watch the comedy . . . and coming back the following Sunday for worship. But *why*?

Because comedy is a powerful – though still under-used – evangelistic tool. Comedy provides the perfect opportunity for churches, ministries and other organizations to build each other up in Christ and attract non-Christians. Laughter is a unique and effective weapon for outreach, team-building and entertainment. It's a great vehicle for reaching out to the community, for four main reasons:

1. Comedy has *universal appeal*. Unlike more subjective media (specific musical styles, drama, etc.), *everyone* enjoys comedy.
2. Comedy *crosses boundaries* – generational, cultural, gender, and especially secular barriers.

3. Comedy *lowers guards*. When people laugh together, they are more receptive to new ideas.
4. Comedy is *unifying*. Laughter opens the door to influential relationships, building a shared bond and positive memories.

Comedy as evangelism is not about trivializing the Gospel. It's about breaking down fuzzy, preconceived stereotypes, and demonstrating the joy of faith through laughter. Jesus was the greatest anecdotalist of them all, and his scathingly satirical take on authority and sin was closer to the ethos of stand-up than you might perceive.

Dr Virginia Trooper says, 'When the mouth is open for laughter, you may be able to shove in a little food for thought.' What I see, very clearly, is a new 'ministry' being created within the world of comedy. And it's a ministry that is not aimed primarily at 'converting atheists into believers', as Kanye West said, but simply at breaking down barriers – changing people's perceptions of what it means to have a faith, and thereby reducing the cynicism that surrounds that faith.

Only three years ago, on the national comedy circuit, there were fewer than five openly Christian performers. That number has grown disproportionately, and there are now well over a dozen – the majority of whom have won awards of some prestige and been touted as stars of the future. The likes of Paul Kerensa, Gareth Richards, Nathan Caton and myself have all received critical acclaim from various quarters, and I haven't even mentioned the fabulous Jo Enright (*Phoenix Nights* and *I'm Alan Partridge*) or the majestic Milton Jones – not that he needs me to!

Even within the dark crevices of showbiz, God is sending out his envoys – his champions. As a consequence, the future of the Body of Christ in this nation looks very bright – because it's growing a funny bone!

It says in the Bible that it's God's will that 'none should perish'. That means he needs Christians to use their gifts in every area of society, and laughter is capable of permeating even the darkest corners of our world. After all, the whole world is a stage, and comedy, done properly, thrives not on façade, but on truth.

God is a laughing God – I'm convinced of it! Our Father's laughter fills the universe – a laugh of exuberance, of triumphant joy, of sheer pleasure in the works of his hands. It is the laugh of a Creator who delights in his creation more than we can possibly comprehend, and who wants us to share in his delight.

God weeps over sin. He is enraged over injustice. He feels deeply our grief and suffering. God knows the full scope of emotion in a way only he can. He is eternal, and tears and joy dwell together in his heart. But we focus so much on the lost-ness of this world that I wonder whether we at all understand and embrace the implications of redemption. Laughter – God's laughter – reigned in the beginning. In the end, it will swallow up all sorrow and darkness. And mark this: in these times between, God is still the Laughing God.

Every time a baby's face creases in a smile that fills our own heart with laughter and love, somewhere out of sight but very, very close at hand, our Father is laughing too – tenderly, joyously. He simply loves to laugh. It is what he is about. And when you get a group of people laughing together with joy, I believe you get an idea of how God wanted things to be. Because all the grim realities of life in this fallen world ultimately will not win out over the laughter of God.

Andy Kind
www.emergingculture.co.uk
www.isaacproject.co.uk

Andy Dipper

REPRESENTING
THE POLITICAL
JESUS

Jesus entered the temple area and began driving out those who were buying and selling there. . . .

Mark 11:15, NIV

Andy Dipper is the Chief Executive of Release International, an organization that supports the persecuted Church and campaigns on their behalf to bring freedom of worship and basic human rights to Christians all over the world. They, and others working alongside them, represent the political Jesus.

A few months after the Taliban had taken power in Kabul, Afghanistan, I found myself nervously taking off my shoes and respectfully lowering my head as I entered the Ministry of the Interior Passport Office in Kabul's city centre. Power and authority greeted me in the form of a turban-wearing man in his late teens sprawled over a broken metal desk, scowling at me and demanding my visa application papers. Interrogation regarding my work and activities eventually led to my passport being thrown back to me with the requisite visa inside, which would last me for the following twelve weeks. All foreigners repeatedly went through this process, with this young Taliban wielding his power to reject any application if he wished. We had no rights to appeal, for we were 'aliens', having chosen to live and work there, submitting to the government's authority in order to remain. Months later our work was closed down, even though we had been careful to obtain all the permission papers that were required.

Living today in Britain, my family and I enjoy the liberty and freedom which *millions* around the world do not experience. Working for Release International has opened my eyes to the oppression which so many people around the world face on a day-to-day basis. As I meet such people, their life experience does not tend to be one of self-pity or regret, rather one of sober reflection and even celebration. I have the privilege of sitting with them as they reflect on how the Lord has been close to them through the toughest of times, when all is stripped away. I see and hear the way that God's grace and comfort have permeated throughout and carried them through. They readily testify to the fact that more and more people want to know the Lord Jesus for themselves. Growth in the midst of suffering – this sounds odd, but history has shown this to be the norm in countries like China and Burma, amongst many others.

But let us consider Human Rights. Tolerance, mutual respect, equality, harmony – all valuable aspirations in community building, but are they realistic and even possible around the world today? Following the Second

World War, great efforts were made to promote peace and understanding between nations. Article 18 of the United Nations Declaration of Human Rights states:

Everyone has the right to freedom of thought, conscience and religion; this right includes freedom to change his religion or belief, and freedom, either alone or in community with others and in public or private, to manifest his religion or belief in teaching, practice, worship and observance.[1]

Whilst member states signed up to the Declaration, full adoption of these aspirational statements still has not been achieved around the world. In many countries they are officially enshrined in law, yet the reality is somewhat different.

China

Article 36 of China's constitution states:

Citizens of the People's Republic of China enjoy freedom of religious belief. No state organ, public organisation or individual may compel citizens to believe in, or not to believe in, any religion; nor may they discriminate against citizens who believe in, or do not believe in, any religion. The state protects normal religious activities. No one may make use of religion to engage in activities that disrupt public order, impair the health of citizens or interfere with the educational system of the state. Religious bodies and religious affairs are not subject to any foreign domination.[2]

While some improvements have been made regarding religious freedoms, the Chinese government still targets Christians and church leaders, especially from 'unregistered' churches. The Chinese government estimates there are some 20 million Christians in officially registered churches, while those in 'illegal' (unregistered) churches number between 100 million and 150 million, according to different estimates.

There is a clear lack of religious tolerance and freedom for many Christians in China today. The continuing arrest of Christians, the detention of leaders and their imprisonment on contrived charges stand in stark contrast to the more politically and socially developed nation that the government of China wishes to portray.

The fact that a large majority of Christians choose to practise their faith outside of the State-registered church is clear evidence that Chinese Christians object to unnecessary and heavy-handed regulation and control of their peaceful religious activity.

It is encouraging and to be celebrated that there is improved treatment of Christians by the authorities in some parts of China, yet the government in Beijing could do much more to repeal restrictive legislation and to introduce a new era of co-operation, welcoming the positive contribution that Christians can make to the overall development of society.

Let us return to the issue of growth and persecution being related to one another. Two well-respected Chinese Christian leaders in the last few years *support* this idea from their own experience:

Without opposition we will not be as effective as God wants us to be. Without persecution in China there would not have been revival, and without a crucifixion there would not be a resurrection.
Liu Zhenying (better known as Brother Yun)

More persecution, more growing. That's the history of our Church.
Pastor Samuel Lamb

There is an expectation of persecution, not from a desire for self-harm – far from it. What they both know to be true is that when the toughest of pressure is upon them for standing up for their faith in Jesus, God stands with them, remains sovereign and uses their suffering to bring more people into a living *relationship* with him. We shouldn't be surprised, because throughout the Bible we see a picture being painted by Jesus, Peter and Paul. Being a Christian has a price-tag and the name of that price-tag is suffering, as Paul reminds us:

> *If we are distressed, it is for your comfort and salvation; if we are comforted, it is for your comfort, which produces in you patient endurance of the same sufferings we suffer. And our hope for you is firm, because we know that just as you share in our sufferings, so also you share in our comfort.*
>
> 2 Corinthians 1:6–7, NIV

As I watch the Body of Christ and think over this subject, there is something of a paradox emerging here. On one hand there are human rights violations happening in China, and yet also there is the expectation of persecution as the springboard for more people becoming Christians. So, does this mean we should stop campaigning for human rights? Four Christian leaders in Burma showed me that the challenge is for us in the free nations of the world to *keep on* campaigning on behalf of Christians facing oppression, as well as supporting them pastorally and practically as they live through the persecution and take every opportunity to share their living faith with those around them.

Burma

The following is an edited extract from Release International's magazine *Witness*, published after a trip I made in 2007. It enabled many thousands in the British churches to understand more fully the plight of our brothers and sisters in Burma:

> *The Burmese military regime says to be Burmese is to be Buddhist. They describe Christianity as the C-virus. And to make sure*

Burmese children escape that infection, they're removing them from Christian homes and jailing pastors who run orphanages. Burma is a land of many orphans. Needless poverty and equally needless war have taken their toll. Armed conflict rages in several states between ethnic peoples and government troops. The brutality of that violence has appalled the world.

Burma's Tatmadaw *troops have driven thousands into the jungles or across the border, booby-trapping their houses to make sure they can never return. This is a regime that makes use of human minesweepers – villagers driven ahead of troops to trigger waiting landmines. So Burma has more than its fair share of orphans. And many pastors take in abandoned children. But far from offering support, the state closes down these makeshift orphanages, and jails the pastors who run them. Charges range from running an illegal business to human trafficking. But some say the real human traffickers are the authorities themselves, who are dragging away children from the homes of Christians, to bring them up as Buddhists. Pastor Barnabas told me,* 'They want to destroy their faith. The authorities want to convert their faith into Buddhism. So many times they take their children without their parents' permission. They force them into the Buddhist school and they never see their parents again.'

Like many church leaders, Pastor Barnabas also runs a Bible college. There is however no shortage of students willing to risk all to train for the ministry. He led me down a busy side street in the heart of one of Burma's major cities. In this rambling house beside deep open drains students pour in to pray, to worship and to study the Word of God. It's impossible to conceal their activity. The sweetness of their singing drifts like incense through the air. Their survival is down to the Lord's protection and the goodwill of their neighbours. Many roads have government informants, whose job it is to spy on their neighbours and report anything suspicious. It's a charter for corruption. Pastors run a gamut of blackmail and bribery. Those who can't pay could end up rotting for life in a Burmese jail.

What amazed me about the students was their total commitment. With four years of study ahead of them, I asked how they felt about the future. As Christian evangelists the future looked bleak from the perspective of persecution. But these 18–20 year-olds understand that being a Christian today in Burma is just like Jesus explained to his disciples in John 15:20: 'If they persecuted me, they will persecute you also.' There is an inevitable cost in being a Christian – in Jesus' time, today and into the future.

Another Christian that I met, Thomas, was caught by the authorities bringing orphaned children from Chin State so he could care for them more effectively. Instead of offering their support, they jailed him for life. They let Thomas go a month later when his papers were found to be in order. But for that month, Thomas thought he would be behind bars for the rest of his days. And Burmese jails bear scant resemblance to even the most miserable British lock-up. He shared a cell with 70 prisoners and many more mosquitoes. 'Two people took it in turns to wave them away with a cloth. The cell was so crowded we could not lie down to sleep. We had to lie on our sides.'

Almost a quarter of Thomas's fellow prisoners were Christians. The rest were Buddhists. 'The Buddhists have freedom to worship their god, but Christians do not have the same rights as Buddhists. The prison authorities only let us worship for seven minutes.'

And then there was the corruption, which is endemic, even behind bars. 'They asked us for money. When we could not pay they made us clean out the toilet basin used by all the prisoners. And as we cleaned the floor they beat us with sticks. We had no hope but the pastors encouraged us that God was with us.'

Pastor Stephen also risked imprisonment to run an orphanage. The authorities not only closed it down, they forced him to pull it down. So with the help of other church leaders he dismantled his orphanage, carefully, piece by piece, in the hope that one day, the regime might allow him to put it back up. But first they had a special service for the building. 'It was like a funeral service. We invited some of the pastors. They prayed for us and then we just began to dismantle the building. It took about seven days.'

He was forced to split up the 80 children in his care, and today 40 have nowhere to live but a tent. The bitter irony is that the tent is smack in the middle of their former orphanage. But Pastor Stephen's faith is undiminished.

Despite everything, he smiled and said, 'Even if I have been facing problems and hardship in the Lord's ministry, I am not discouraged, because I know that the Lord knows all things. The Lord knows best. He knows when to provide and when to meet all our needs. I just trust the Lord and know that one day the Lord will rebuild everything for his own glory.'

Pastor James found that many Buddhists are converting to Christianity. 'What they say is they have Nirvana – they have peace in their lives as a result of accepting the Lord Jesus Christ.' *Despite everything in the power of the authorities to prevent it, the church is growing.*

'Everywhere we go we see people are receptive to the gospel. In our land, even if we have different kinds of hardship and sufferings, the Lord has been so good to us that he blesses us with spiritual blessings. The more we face problems and the more we face hardship, the more our spiritual life has been growing into maturity. Hardship and problems make us to be perfect in the lives of our ministry.'

Wake up!

Church growth is happening in China and Burma today, and men and women, young and old are risking their liberty and lives to demonstrate the Gospel message. But in stark contrast, nations such as the UK seem almost paralysed, somehow neutralized to the challenge set before all Christians everywhere. In Britain we find Christians with a part-time commitment, having a lukewarm attitude towards Christ and the job of telling others about him. Surely this is missing out on God's plan completely!

The sad reality is that too much of the Church's resources are spent dealing with internal difficulties and divisions, and this in turn distracts us from what God's intentions for us are. In only focusing on ourselves, we can forget the needs of our brothers and sisters around the world. We have a duty to pray and politically campaign for those in the Church who are being persecuted. And our actions can and do make a difference.

The power of positive action and prayer

Helen Berhane is an Eritrean woman, a gifted singer, and a person who in 2004 risked her life by singing Christian songs and making a CD for general distribution in her home country.

That was when the trouble started. She was arrested, locked up in prison and put under massive pressure to sign a statement to deny her faith. She refused, and as a result was beaten severely on her legs and feet over the next two years.

Around the world Helen's story was told in churches and in the press. The lobbying of governments to stand up to President Aferwerki in Eritrea grew and grew.

And what did Release do in all this?

We joined together with other UK-based agencies and launched a petition. We presented 108,000 names to the Eritrean ambassador in July 2006. His response at the time was, 'There is no persecution of Christians in our country.' The evidence suggests otherwise. Today more than 2,000 men and women are in prison in Eritrea simply for being Christians.

As well as the petition, we urged everyone to pray. Amongst many other places, at the Scarborough Easter People conference in 2006, over 150 young people in the Emerging Culture venue prayed. Urged on by Andy Frost and myself, they pressed together in one mass, imagining the pain of being crushed in an overcrowded prison with no escape. We all cried out to God, asking for mercy on those imprisoned in Eritrea, and for President Aferwerki to think again about treating people with such disdain.

God answered in a massive way! Eventually, Helen was released in late 2006 and went into hiding in a country nearby. In October 2007 she was finally granted residence in Denmark. Today, she wants to get on with being a Christian witness right where she is. She is learning Danish, is part of a church, and wants nothing but to give God all the glory!

We were all amazed and thrilled. But Helen reminded me recently that, of course, there are hundreds and hundreds of others who still suffer, who are treated so badly – all simply for being Christians. And so Release International will continue to pray and to campaign on behalf of those whose basic human rights have been taken away.

So, what are you going to do? Visit our website below or give us a call on 01689 823491. Sign up, get the email alerts, download the monthly podcasts with the latest news of what is happening around the world. And stand with us as, together, we stand up for those persecuted for being

Christian in their countries around the world.

Freedom comes to so many of us like a gift, but for millions around the world today there is a high price to be paid for living out a Christian life. Will you stand with us as we stand up for those parts of the Church that need our help?

Andy Dipper
www.releaseinternational.org

1. Universal Declaration of Human Rights (1948) http://www.un.org/Overview/rights.html

2. Constitution of the People's Republic of China (1982, modified 1988, 1993, 1999 & 2004) http://english.gov.cn/2005-08/05/content_20813.htm

Nola Leach

REPRESENTING
THE FAITHFUL
JESUS

Let your 'Yes' be 'Yes', and your 'No', 'No'.
Matthew 5:37, NIV

Nola Leach is the Chief Executive of CARE. They are an organization concerned about the crumbling standards of integrity shown by leaders in all areas of public life, and so seek to support leaders and bring credibility back. In doing this they represent the faithful Jesus.

I was recently challenged by the words of the late President Roosevelt: 'The true Christian is the true citizen; lofty of purpose, resolute in endeavour, ready for a hero's deeds . . . following the higher law . . . and in this world doing all that in him lies, so that when death comes he may feel that mankind is in some degree better because he has lived.'

We live in a world where 'spin' is the order of the day. With relish, many people read the diaries of politicians and policy-makers. Big business corporations, even those with a stated ethos of integrity and openness, fall foul of fraud and embezzlement. It is therefore no wonder that cynicism and apathy abound. No one can be trusted and leaders seem to be the worst. Critics are everywhere. Yet to return to Roosevelt:

> *It's not the critic who counts, nor the man who points out where the strong man stumbled, or how the doer of deeds could have done better. No, the credit belongs to the man who is actually in the arena, whose face is marred by the dust and sweat and blood; who strives valiantly; who errs and comes up short again and again because there is no effort without error or shortcoming; who spends himself in a worthy cause; who, at worst, if he fails, at least fails while daring greatly. Far better is it to do mighty things . . . than to rank with those poor souls who neither enjoy nor suffer, because they dwell in the grey twilight that knows neither victory nor defeat.*

For the Christian, there is no sacred/secular divide. Jesus came to bring life in all its fullness, and it is the duty and privilege of every Christian to be God's representative, a steward over his creation. We need look no further than Genesis 1 to discover that God's 'creation mandate' demands that we get involved in the world around us. Christian faith encompasses every aspect of life and calls for involvement in all areas of society today. In the same way as a small pinch of salt diffuses flavour throughout a whole meal, so the Christian brings God's cleansing into the blackest areas. As light illuminates the darkest of places, so the follower of Jesus brings God's light, giving guidance and safety.

Today many of our country's leaders are motivated by working for the good of their community. I am mindful of the MP whose response to seeing poverty at first hand in the developing world was to enter politics; the cross-party group of MPs looking at what the Christian response should be to what Britain might look like in 2020; the MPs from all parties who meet to pray and support each other; and the many Christian MPs who are practically cared for by Christians in their constituencies.

There are many examples of Christians working to transform the communities in which they live. It is my privilege to work for the Christian charity CARE, which exists to clearly declare the truth about God and demonstrate his compassion for those he has made. In practice this means supporting and equipping Christians and policy-makers to uphold justice and care for the vulnerable for the good of individuals and their communities. On the wall of our offices is a print of the famous painting of William Wilberforce. Here is an inspirational man. A man who saw an injustice, the slave trade, and devoted his life to work with others to destroy it. It has been noted elsewhere that Wilberforce brought to political life a good education; he was articulate, well informed and compassionate; a man of deep integrity. So were many of his contemporaries. What marked him out was his decision to embrace Christianity. It redefined how he saw humanity – all men were made in the image of God.

Where are the Wilberforces of today?

It is our privilege to work with many in the public sphere whose public service stems from their belief in Christ. It is refreshing to listen to the stories of how their faith is the motivating factor behind all they do.

Political life

People like Adam. He can trace his journey into public service back to his childhood. A formative moment for him was when his father was fired by the BBC. A shop steward, he had led the fight for better pay for his members. It was a hard time. Money was short, and for the first time, Adam realized that other people could decide what standard of living his family might have. People with no apparent connection to them could make decisions that would have a dramatic impact on their lives.

Adam's father's passion to fight injustice in the work-place was an ethic he imparted strongly to his son – the idea that corporately people can do more, that individuals can be empowered. Adam's father's attitude to the Government of the day was understandably aggressive. As Adam's own ideas took shape, family meal-times were very lively.

On 22 November 1990, Margaret Thatcher resigned as Prime Minister. As he, along with millions of others, watched her car leave Downing Street, Adam decided that he wanted to be involved in the political life of the UK. Because he had become convinced that the individual did matter, and especially to God, he became involved in party politics. He believed that by working with others, individuals could become empowered to change families and communities.

The next highly formative period was when, after reading politics at university, he was accepted onto the CARE Intern Programme. CARE takes young graduates and aims to equip them with the tools they need to engage effectively as Christians within a secular culture. CARE Interns benefit from the unique experience of integrating cutting-edge Christian thinking with practical hands-on activities. Over 150 graduates are now working in positions of influence around the world.

During Adam's year he worked with the then shadow Secretary of State for International Development. This gave him a view of the world outside of the UK and the challenges to be faced. It was the experiences of this year which equipped him for his job in Northamptonshire, where he is now the Leadership Support Manager (or Chief of Staff) at Northamptonshire County Council, supporting the Chief Executive and the Leader of the Council in the carrying out of their duties across Northamptonshire, at both regional and national level.

Adam believes public service is an honour, working each day on behalf of a community to help them in so many ways – running the schools service, providing social services to adults and children, looking after children who do not have parents or suitable family support, building and maintaining roads, commissioning and developing and investing in the voluntary sector.

He thinks long and hard about leadership in the public square. He believes that there is One higher than us whom we serve. When he was choosing a career, it struck him that he could be a doctor and help people. He could be a policeman or a teacher. What drew him towards politics was the question, 'What are you building?' It is like two men chiselling stone; you ask them what they are doing. One man might say in response, 'I'm chiselling stone'; the other, 'I'm building a cathedral.' Two men doing the same thing but with two different views of how important their activity is. Adam wants to leave a legacy, something lasting longer than he will, helping people long after he has died.

It is interesting that Adam's attitude to public life drove him to become a school governor and then a chair of governors. Being a Christian made a difference. Looking back on his time as a school governor led him to believe that this is one of the most important areas where society can be influenced for good: being a member of a body of about twelve people, running a school, appointing heads and teachers, setting policies relating to issues like sex education, budgets, buildings and discipline; working on behalf of a future generation.

School governance

More and more Christians are taking up the challenge to influence their local schools for good in this way. Not all have a degree in politics, as Adam does. Julie had no higher education. A single parent, she was concerned about certain issues in the school her daughter attended, and instead of complaining, she sought to do something positive. To begin with, she joined the Parent Teacher Association and helped by running events, raising money and getting to know the staff and their needs. She was then asked to stand as the parent representative on the governing body. At first she thought that she would not be up to the task, but her church encouraged her and she took up the challenge. Julie now helps with the training of other governors and sees it as a real privilege to be involved in supporting often stressed staff and sharing in the shaping of young lives.

Of course, it is not just in politics that Christians see their calling to transform society. Businessmen are often seen as being intent on making money solely for themselves. However, there are many Christians who see the business world as the area into which God has called them. The way they work honours him as they seek to build a society for the benefit of others.

The business world

Michael is one such man. He runs a small business in the construction industry. He sees his life in the business world as a blessing from God. He believes that as he is blessed, he should also be a blessing to others. This is more than a financial blessing (for shareholders, employees, loan providers, customers, sub-contractors) but also spills over into how he treats people. It is easy to talk about principles of integrity and valuing people, but this has to be worked out in practice. Therefore Michael's team endeavour to pay all of their bills on time (and even early, if possible), and they pay their employees and sub-contractors before themselves. They do not twist the truth and would rather under-promise and over-deliver than promise to do something and then not be able to achieve it. A great deal of time and effort is put into developing and training staff, and they are not just regarded as nine-to-five employees. On more than one occasion the management have provided personal loans when staff have been in financial difficulty – in one case stopping the bailiffs from repossessing an employee's house with less than fifteen minutes to spare! The houses that they build are houses that the management would like to live in, finished to a standard that they would be happy with.

At a wider level, they look holistically at business ventures. They desire to make not only a financial profit, but also a social profit. They look carefully at every opportunity that comes their way, and not just in terms of 'How much money can it make us?' Their desire is to be involved in a range of business ventures where they are able to provide business capital and experience to people who have a great idea and passion, but not the money or experience to make it a reality. Some of these projects would be for profit and some would be more angled towards a social benefit.

The work of the business is undergirded by prayer and the expectation of what a just and loving God is going to do. Michael and his team are supported by a prayer group from their church.

As they have sought to honour God in all their business dealings, they have found that the Lord has given them tremendous favour with bankers, contractors, advisors, investors and buyers – far beyond what their years, experience and reputation merit. Together with their church, they plan to stay on their knees, no matter how well things go!

Politics has been defined as 'the art of living together in community'. Those who claim to follow Jesus Christ are part of God's people living in God's world. If we look back into the history of the Jews, God's people, there was a time when they were in exile in Babylon. One of their leaders was Nehemiah, a man who felt he was called to 'work for the blessing of the city'. Today there are Christians up and down the land who are doing just this.

Developing prayer networks

Much is written about disaffected young people and the growth in vandalism. A few years ago a group of Christian young people got together because of their concern for the repeated attacks on their school in the heart of Glasgow. They decided to get together to pray. With the faith of young people, they believed that God would act. When a (perhaps) more cynical adult asked them what happened, their response was so refreshing: 'We prayed, God acted and the vandalism stopped.'

Inspired by their example, the Schools Prayer Network was born, with the vision that every school in the UK should become a prayed-for school. The Network involves parents, staff, pupils, local churches, and Christian friends. There are now thousands of groups across the UK working with their local schools, praying intelligently and practically on a regular basis.

Groups have been operating for many years with exciting results. One such group prayed for a student who was critically ill with a brain tumour. After a long battle he recovered. He has since become a Christian and attends a local church.

Another group has reported that the head of their state school has recently agreed to have a 'prayer box' at the school for prayer requests from children, teachers and parents. 'Our school prayer group currently only meets monthly,' said the group's representative, 'but we may need to pray about specific prayer requests on a more regular basis.'

One teacher wrote to the Network to say: 'We have witnessed a steady outpouring from God onto the school. This has enabled us to be more ambitious in our prayers and to ask in faith. I would urge all who pray for schools to be encouraged and keep going.'

Supporting individuals, changing policies

From its beginning, the Christian Church has been marked out by its care for those in need, and still today thousands of Christians daily exhibit God's love in action.

Abortion has been much in the news recently, with the fortieth anniversary of the 1967 Abortion Act. For those involved, this is always a painful situation. For many years, under the auspices of CareConfidential, trained volunteers have been providing care and support for individual women in crisis pregnancy situations, or for those who are struggling after an abortion. Over twenty years, hundreds of thousands of women have been helped, each of them respected as an individual loved by God and presented sensitively with truths about the choices they face. Whilst the focus remains on helping individual women, if change is to be effected so that women are fully supported when facing this kind of situation, then the systems and structures in our society that fail to take account of the harm done to the mother and child by abortion need to be influenced for good. The Christian crisis pregnancy movement recognizes that we cannot just sit and wait for people in need to come for help.

Christians concerned about these issues could choose the option of waving placards outside Parliament, abortion clinics, hospitals or schools, pointing the finger and criticizing. A far better option at a practical and personal level is to get involved, to engage with 'the world' but not to be 'of the world'.

Many pregnancy centres affiliated to CareConfidential go into schools to give lessons in sex and relationships education and take part in local teenage pregnancy forums. Because of their reputation for excellence, one centre's schools team leader has been invited to provide sexual health training for all sexual health educators in her county! Centres are also being asked to run counselling services in hospitals where gynaecologists are recognizing that some of their patients are still ambivalent and obviously upset at the proposed abortion.

One advisor wrote: 'The nurses themselves now send away women to rethink their decision if they feel they are at all unsure. We thank God for the relationships our advisors have built with the nurses and the positive impact that our presence has made. They also want us to do more staff training with both clinic and ward nurses.'

There is much talk today about tolerance in society. As Christians we cannot tolerate evil, but that does not give us permission to repay evil with evil! Instead, we must confront the dilemmas with mercy and love.

Conclusion

Abraham Kuyper, theologian and Prime Minister of the Netherlands from 1901 to 1905, wrote: 'In the total expanse of human life there is not a single square inch of which Christ, who alone is sovereign, does not declare, "That is mine!"'

This powerful thought is clearly taught throughout the Bible. John's Gospel says of Jesus: 'Through him all things were made; without him nothing was made that has been made' (1:3, NIV). The writer to the Hebrews talks of him 'sustaining all things by his powerful word' (1:3, NIV). This means that there is no sacred/secular divide. God is already here. The illustrations in this chapter speak loudly of the fact that in the places of greatest need, God's people are revealing his light, perspective and wisdom.

Nola Leach
www.care.org.uk

Daleep Mukarji

REPRESENTING
THE ECO-WARRIOR
JESUS

The earth is the LORD's, and everything in it.

Psalm 24:1, NIV

Daleep Mukariji is the director of Christian Aid, one of the organizations leading the way in the fight against climate change. In doing so they represent the eco-warrior Jesus.

*And they were all filled with the Holy Spirit and spoke the word of
God boldly.*

Acts 4:31, NIV

*We definitely have more hurricanes and floods than we used to. I've
lived here all my life and it wasn't like this before. Strong winds and
big waves from the sea cause more floods now.*

Dominica Echevarría (aged 29), from El Salvador

In common with other development agencies, Christian Aid has for many
years worked on disaster risk reduction in parts of the world that are
particularly vulnerable to extreme weather, especially the poor countries in
central America and the Caribbean. This kind of work includes helping
people to make their houses secure against hurricanes and floods, and
training them in procedures that can save their lives when disaster strikes.

In recent years it has become evident that these emergencies are
occurring more often and with greater intensity. Moïse Jean Paul, from the
Environment Ministry in Haiti, comments: 'It is clear that hurricanes have
been hitting the island more often and with much more force over the past
decade.' And while most of the people directly affected have no specialist
knowledge of global warming and its causes, they are in little doubt that
the weather is changing.

What is particularly significant about these observations from El
Salvador and Haiti is that they come from people in two of the poorest
countries in the world. So by definition, the people already being seriously
affected by global warming are those least able to cope with it.

The injustice of climate change

While our work in disaster-prone regions is vitally important in helping poor
people to protect themselves and their livelihoods in the face of extreme
weather events, this is not the main reason why climate change is a top

priority for Christian Aid. It is now well known and widely accepted that it is the carbon emissions of people in developed countries that have brought about the present crisis. Indeed, the inequality between countries in the global North and those in the global South is well summed up in their estimated *per capita* carbon emissions: between 10 and 12 tonnes for someone living in western Europe, 24 tonnes for a US citizen, and less than 1 tonne for a family living in Zambia.

While people in northern Europe may feel that a temperature rise of a few degrees is not unwelcome, those further south are threatened with losing their livelihoods and even losing their lives. When the temperature rose to around 48 degrees in Delhi, the rickshaw drivers, among the poorest people in the city, had no choice but to keep working in the heat, and many died. When a farmer in Nicaragua found that the rainy season was up to two months late, he lost the possibility of harvesting two crops of beans in a year, which was essential if he was to feed his family. So he went off to Costa Rica to work illegally on the coffee plantations for half the year instead. Climate change has forced him to risk imprisonment and so jeopardize his family's survival.

People living in the global South are worst affected by climate change and at the same time they have done least to cause the problem. And because poor people will always suffer more than the rich in any disaster, however it is caused, it is not hard to see that climate change impacts directly on the two key aims of a Christian development agency: to alleviate poverty and to challenge injustice.

There is another reason why climate change should be regarded as a justice issue. It comes at a time when the world's richest nations have reached a peak of development while the poorest are still struggling to get onto the development ladder. While it is well within the means of rich countries both to maintain their current levels of economic activity and to adapt to climate change, the picture is very different for poor countries.

Justice demands that the development of poor countries should continue, and this will present a challenge to the global North, not least in the greater investment required of us while at the same time changing our own industrial habits. People in the developing world must be supported as they confront extreme heat, floods and so on, and yet their development must continue in an environmentally sustainable way, that is likely to draw on all the new and evolving technologies of developed countries.

Climate change and Scripture

Christian Aid is the official development agency of 41 Protestant denominations, and as such our concern for poverty and injustice, and the actions we take as a result, is firmly rooted in the Bible.

The principles of caring for the vulnerable people in society and of seeking justice for those who have been wronged find early expression in the Old Testament law books designed for an emerging theocratic state. The Book of Deuteronomy sets the duty to care for 'the stranger, the orphan and the widow' alongside commonsense obligations to follow good agricultural practices and the humanitarian command to grant, every seventh year, relief of debt and freedom for slaves.

In the New Testament, such duties become more than regulations for a healthy society. Jesus' announcement at the start of his ministry, that he has come to 'bring good news to the poor' and to 'let the oppressed go free' (Luke 4:18), expresses the essence of the incarnation: the Son of God himself has become poor and will suffer oppression. So when he reveals to his followers how the Son of Man will return in glory, Jesus (now as King) tells them, 'I was sick and you looked after me, I was in prison and you came to visit me', because 'whatever you did for one of the least of these . . . you did for me' (Matt. 25:36, 40, NIV). Our work is not undertaken out of religious obligation. Rather, it is a response of solidarity that is faithful to the example of Jesus Christ.

Our theology is the same, whether we're dealing with HIV/AIDS, trade justice or the effects of climate change. And a model that is particularly helpful when we confront these complex contemporary issues is one based on relationships.

Christian environmentalism has done much to highlight the biblical relationships between God, human beings and the created world. It is a very ancient part of Christian tradition that nature reveals something of God to humanity, in particular God's goodness and beauty: 'The heavens declare the glory of God; the skies proclaim the work of his hands' (Ps. 19:1, NIV). On a practical level, the Old Testament also talks about caring for the land. And throughout the Bible we see how human rebellion against God is reflected in natural devastation (such as the drought in Judah in Jer. 14), while reconciliation translates into abundance (Isa. 55).

Yet the crisis of climate change demands that we take another relationship into account: that between human beings themselves. In Luke 10, Jesus asks a lawyer how he understands the law, to which the man replies, '"Love the Lord your God with all your heart . . ."; and, "Love your neighbour as yourself"' (Luke 10:27, NIV). This is the crucial teaching underlying the parable of the Good Samaritan that answers the question, 'Who is my neighbour?' To love God is to love his creation. In the context of climate change, to love our neighbour is to care for the people we have damaged while we were harming God's creation, albeit unwittingly. 'Do this', says Jesus, 'and you will live' (Luke 10:28, NIV).

Importantly, the New Testament offers the hope that broken relationships can be mended and a damaged world healed. The ministry of Jesus shows us that this is not some kind of pious hope for the distant future, but a promise for the here and now. So it is important that we understand the vision of a 'new heaven and a new earth' in Revelation 21 as a promise for our time as well as for future generations. Just as the resurrection body of Jesus bore the marks of suffering, so our new earth will be scarred by some irreversible damage: dried-up rivers, new expanses of desert, areas rendered uninhabitable by extreme heat. Yet we have the potential to heal. We can mend our relationship with the natural world by drastically reducing our emissions of carbon dioxide. We have it in our power to say, 'This far and no further.' The challenge is to find the will to respond, as our theology shows us we must.

Action is a key message of the resurrection. If we look at the Gospel accounts of Jesus' resurrection appearances, we see that in most cases their purpose is twofold: they convey the information that Jesus has risen from the dead, and they also command us to act – feed my lambs (John 21:15), go and make disciples (Matt. 28:19), forgive people's sins (John 20:23). In other words, the hope of the resurrection is not something for us to keep to ourselves; we must pass it on to others, especially now the millions of people affected by poverty and global warming, by taking the necessary actions to address their needs.

Speaking out and taking action

With evidence from around the world that temperatures are rising and weather patterns becoming increasingly unpredictable, it is all too easy to believe that there is nothing we can do to affect an increasingly bleak future. The good news is that for most of us it's not too late. The bad news is that within a few decades it may well be, and that for some of the poorest people in the world the outlook even today is very bleak. So the initial challenge is to accept that the need to act is urgent. We can't afford to wait for more conferences, debates or synodical resolutions.

This is, of course, the message of Pentecost. The gift of the Holy Spirit brought instantaneous results – no hanging around and forming committees to decide who was to be the spokesperson and to consider the best time to do it. As tongues of fire rested on the disciples, 'All of them were filled with the Holy Spirit and began to speak in other tongues as the Spirit enabled them' (Acts 2:4, NIV).

The gift of the Spirit was not only immediate, it was for everyone. So another challenge is for everyone to speak out on climate change and to take action, not to leave it to someone else who is better at it. Coupled with this is the urgent need for us to make changes in our own lifestyles, if we are not to make a bad situation still worse.

Christian Aid's campaign, 'Climate changed', makes some strong demands on governments and business leaders, who are the people best placed to bring about effective change. It is pushing for a minimum of 80 per cent cuts in carbon emissions by 2050 by all the world's richest nations, which is the equivalent of a 5 per cent cut every year. This is a big challenge and not something that any one organization can achieve on its own. But most of us are voters, investors, consumers, employees, and we all have a voice that we can use to influence decision-makers in politics and business.

Politicians listen to the voices of the people who elect them to office, and they will use their influence in government, in Europe and worldwide. The corporate sector also has a huge part to play. While the United Kingdom's total carbon emissions amount to just 2 per cent of global emissions, that rises to 12 or 15 per cent once companies' international activities are taken into account. Unless business leaders hear the voices of the people who buy their products, they have little incentive to change their practices.

We can all speak out against climate change and make a difference to people whose lives depend on it. And we can add to that changes in our own lifestyle so that by reducing our carbon footprint, also by 5 per cent year on year, we don't make a bad situation even worse.

The target of reducing carbon emissions by 80 per cent by 2050 is, we believe, no more than is necessary to halt the damage to God's world and to keep the rise in global temperatures to no more than two degrees. And even then we must recognize that for some people that rise is lethal and will force them to seek refuge in a place where temperatures are lower.

Continuing development

Despite this urgency, in Sub-Saharan Africa climate change is seen as just one more problem by people already struggling under the burden of unfair trade, HIV and poverty. The Human Development Index for 2005 showed that the bottom 24 countries (out of 177) were all in this region. Here, more than anywhere, it is vital that development work continues and increases.

In Burkina Faso, the Revd Elie Kabore became aware of global warming around five years ago. 'The sun is hotter than before – it burns on the skin. It was never that way before. It was 2002 when it first dawned on me that this was the case, that there was a change.' Before that, Pastor Kabore, who had spent a number of years away from his homeland as a student, had become aware, on returning to Burkina in 1978, that it didn't rain as much as it had previously. In his village of Koungou the lack of rain had a devastating effect on agriculture and all the wells that were dug soon dried up. The situation was rescued by Christian Aid's partner organization, ODE (the French abbreviation stands for Evangelical Development Organization). They built a dam to maintain the water supply and Pastor Kabore, who has horticultural training, has been able to introduce people to hitherto unfamiliar crops – potatoes, cauliflower and broccoli. Importantly, people now produce vegetables in both the dry and rainy seasons, resulting in two harvests per year instead of one.

But while projects like this will mitigate some of the worst effects of climate change, much bigger ones are needed if the country is also to develop significantly and in an appropriate way. In Ouagadougou, the capital of Burkina, Christian Aid is supporting a Swiss organization, the Albert Schweitzer Ecological Centre (CEAS), that is working with local people to create technology appropriate to their needs. So, for example, in one of the city's maternity hospitals, CEAS is harnessing solar power for water heaters and refrigerators. There is the obvious advantage that the hospital is now able to create a sterile environment and there are no electricity bills at the end of the month. The downside is the cost of the heaters themselves, and the fact that the government is unlikely to promote solar power while there is a state monopoly of the mains electricity supply. So the problem for the poorest people in a poor country remains a complex one.

There are also hard choices to be made. Do we continue to support Kenyan growers who export their flowers to Europe by air? Or do we save the air miles and deprive them of their livelihoods? Early casualties of the biofuels initiative were Brazilian sugar producers who lost their income once sugar-beet was used to produce fuel instead. In addressing such issues, development specialists are conscious that they may need to do things very differently in the future if people in poor countries are to continue to develop as global carbon emissions fall.

Working together

It is a key principle of development that people should be empowered to help themselves without becoming dependent on outside intervention. Despite the unequal burden that climate change imposes on people across the world, it is becoming clear that poor communities in vulnerable regions are themselves working to reduce the impact of global warming.

In many countries the effects of extreme weather have been made worse by deforestation. And local communities are often heavily involved in replacing trees that have been cut down for a variety of reasons. Abdoulaye Diack from Senegal is one person who has completely changed his views in the light of environmental damage and climate change. He used to cut down trees for construction work, to make charcoal and to feed his cattle, and he admits, 'I am among those who have destroyed the land.' But having learnt about the importance of trees in helping to prevent drought in his region, he is anxious to pass that knowledge on. 'When you plant one tree, even just one, you are reviving the land. I hope the seed we are planting today will help to bless future generations.'

Elsewhere the situation is more complex. Deforestation in neighbouring Honduras causes the Honduran river to flood in El Salvador. In El Salvador itself, it is typically the wealthy who break the law and cut down mangrove trees to build houses and make luxury furniture. In some cases landowners cut down forests and plant sugar-cane instead. Yet small communities who make a living by selling the crabs that live in the mangrove swamps and who need to protect their water supply are busy replanting trees to safeguard their future.

Climate change has been unfairly inflicted on poor countries by the rich North. While in some communities people are working together to mitigate its effects, this does not negate the responsibility of the polluters of the North to reduce their future carbon emissions and also to compensate countries in the South for the damage they have caused.

The task, then, of a Church that is active outside its own walls is to remain true to our calling to love God and love our neighbour, recognizing that in the face of the climate change crisis, such love may take unfamiliar forms. But when we speak out on behalf of those worst affected and take action that may prove to be costly, we will be able to say with St Paul, 'by faith we eagerly await through the Spirit the righteousness for which we hope' (Gal. 5:5, NIV).

Dr Daleep Mukariji
www.christianaid.org.uk

Jonathan Clark

REPRESENTING
THE RELATIONAL
JESUS

*They devoted themselves
. . . to the fellowship.*

Acts 2:42, NIV

**Jonathan Clark is the manager of Premier Radio's Lifeline
service, which provides a sense of community and relationships
for many who would otherwise be lonely. In doing this he and his
colleagues represent the relational Jesus.**

We were all called into the downstairs back office to hear an announcement. The Managing Director had something important to tell the team. I was a temp doing some summer work between school and university, and went with the rest of the staff. The boss was Peter Meadows and the organization was Buzz Christian Ministries, best known for the publication *Buzz Magazine*. This was 1980 and it was the summer when *Family Magazine* was being launched.

So what was it that the boss wanted to say? That day he announced that he felt God was calling him to focus his time and attention on the establishment of a Christian radio station in the United Kingdom. The challenge was immense. Trans World Radio had been broadcasting English-language programmes from Monte Carlo for many years, but these were only available for a few minutes a day on the medium wave, unless you bought a specialist short-wave radio. The Government had made it legally impossible to have a religious radio station based and broadcasting in the United Kingdom. Was this a reaction to what was perceived as the excesses of some of the overseas radio and television religious programmes? Whatever the reason, the law in the UK would be the first of many challenges to overcome before applying for a radio licence to broadcast.

The news from the boss came as a surprise, a shock to many; he was changing the direction of his energies. Knowing all he had achieved to date and his determined nature, few in that room doubted that he would succeed, but it would need a great deal of prayer and a miracle for it to come to fruition.

As I look back over nearly three decades, I have often reflected on how important the Christian music scene and *Buzz Magazine* were to the Christian community and especially the young people of the time. As I sit in the offices of Premier Christian Radio, I can fully understand how the vision for a Christian radio station was an extension of the role of the magazines to strengthen the Christian community. It was seeking to reach out to people through the medium of the airwaves to touch their lives in a deep and personal way.

This article is not a history of Premier Christian Radio, so suffice it to say that on 10 June 1995, after a change in the law and one failed licence application, Premier Christian Radio launched in Battersea Park in London. The vision given by God and announced in that back-office meeting came to fulfilment fifteen years later.

I went to university and moved away from the London suburbs. I was aware, through the Christian grapevine, of the campaign and moves towards Christian radio. Later I returned to live in Surrey, but when Premier was launched, I found I was living beyond the official broadcast area of the M25, and reception was limited at best and poor in the evenings. I never lost interest in radio and always remembered the conviction of the vision that Peter Meadows had when he made the announcement.

In April 1998 God clearly spoke to me in a way I could not ignore. He challenged me as to why I did not listen to Premier. The easy answer was that the reception was poor, but I did as I was told and started listening to Premier in the mornings, in particular *Focus on the Family* with James Dobson. Within a week, at the end of *Focus on the Family*, I heard an advert: 'Are you . . .' followed by a list of experience and skills. I looked at my wife and she at me. It was as if someone was reading out my life experience. It was the advert for the manager of Lifeline. I was about to start a six months' secondment from my job, and God timed it so that as soon as this was completed, I went to work for Premier.

I had always been interested in radio, and had known about radio stations that not only broadcasted to a population but also became an integral part of the life of that community. Premier is one of those radio stations. It is not a local radio station in the same geographical sense as many of the others, but its roots in the Christian community give it that feel.

The founders had incorporated a response mechanism to interact with the listeners. This was not just the ability to telephone the studio for phone-ins or competitions, but a strategic plan for a fully operational community unit called Lifeline, with a team of trained volunteers available to answer the calls of listeners. Callers could ask about programmes, guests and music as they would with other radio stations, but in addition they could ask for prayer, find a listening ear, talk about issues of faith and be signposted to numerous other resources. There was also a range of materials on relevant subjects that could be sent out.

Lifeline was designed to be a Christian-based helpline combining the features of a media response, an emotional support, and information with a Christian enquiry and prayer line. This mix is its strength and its challenge. The volunteers on Lifeline do not know what the next call might be and have to be prepared for anything. One moment they might deal with an enquiry regarding a song or a guest, and the next they may receive a call from someone who is questioning whether to go on living.

We try to answer everything that comes in, but there have been occasions when it would have taken a miracle to find the right answer, such as: 'What was the name of the song played last week which had the words "Holy" or "God" in its title?' or 'Can you tell me the name of the evangelist featured on Premier last summer?' I compare it to being like a detective, where there are a limited number of clues, often inconclusive, sometimes contradictory, and frequently misleading, and the team try their utmost to find the answer.

'So, who can be a Lifeliner?' This is a question I am regularly asked, often with the expectation that you have to be professionally qualified to work on Lifeline. In fact, it is almost the opposite. Anyone can apply to be a Lifeliner. There are neither age restrictions nor denominational conditions. There are no specified qualifications except a willingness to agree to the ethos and statement of faith of Lifeline. We offer a service to the whole

Christian community and beyond, and it is essential that everyone undergoes the same training and understands the underlying principles of Lifeline. With volunteers from across the whole church spectrum, our training challenges preconceived ideas and denominational biases.

Lifeliners also have to be able to observe the strict confidentiality rules of Lifeline. We have a policy of maintaining the anonymity of the caller by using only the first name. There is no record of the caller's telephone number and we have a non-tracing policy so that they can be assured of calling without any risk of identification.

The principle we follow is two-fold. Firstly, everyone who calls retains responsibility for themselves and their actions. If they need to call a third party, whether this is the hospital or the police, then they are encouraged to take this action themselves. Furthermore, we believe as a Christian helpline that we have access to God in prayer and can hand the person into his care. Even if there is nothing more we can do, he can intervene in ways beyond our expectation. Over the years we have known God do amazing things in this regard.

One example of this was someone who had taken an overdose, called Lifeline, spoke to us for a while and then dropped the call. A few days later we heard that minutes after the caller dropped the call, their doorbell rang and it was a friend from church who had been given a clear conviction by God in their spirit that they had to go and visit this person urgently. The person received help and was also reassured that God knew their desperation and sent someone to them.

One regularly heard comment is, 'I have Premier on every radio in my house and I listen all day and all night.' For many listeners, Premier is truly their family. For those who are housebound, isolated, or limited in social contacts, Premier becomes an integral part of their life and social networks.

Radio is still a unique medium, listened to almost anywhere. We can have radios in every room in the house as well as the garden and the car.

We will have the radio on whilst doing a complete range of activities and therefore will feel a close kinship with the presenters. Who else would you have in the bedroom and bathroom with you?!

Many listeners describe Premier as a key or even a core part of their life. We do not want to encourage people to rely solely on Premier, and instead direct them to find Christian fellowship through local church involvement. However, for those who are restricted to the home setting, Premier and Lifeline may become a key aspect of their support network; for example, those limited by age, infirmity or mental illness. Premier can bring the teaching and worship of the Church to the person at home. The friendly known voices of presenters greet the person when they wake and stay with them until they go to sleep, and for those who find it hard to sleep, Premier is there for them during the night as well. Lifeline offers a human point of contact from 9 a.m. to midnight every day of the year, including Christmas and New Year.

I am often asked if Christmas is a busy time of year for Lifeline calls, and to the surprise of many, my answer is that it is generally a quieter time. For Christians, Christmas is busy with the distractions of carol services, nativity plays, cards, decorations, family, and so forth. There is a change in the type of call that comes in over Christmas and New Year. The quantity may reduce but the intensity of need often increases.

Festivals tend to focus our minds on friends, family, memories, hopes and dreams. They are seen to be a time of joy, but for some they are when the loss of a loved one is reinforced, or when depression feels even worse, as others seem to be having a wonderful time and the gap is like an abyss. Lifeline is a friendly voice at the end of the telephone, a voice of hope. It can also be a voice of peace when a parent is overwhelmed by the demands of the children fighting over a broken toy!

I believe that times of national distress and trauma are when Premier and Lifeline can serve and mobilize the community most effectively. Just a few years after the launch of Premier, the death of Diana, Princess of Wales, shocked young and old people alike. Premier responded to this in a sensitive way on air and by opening Lifeline for extended hours and giving people a chance to talk about their feelings.

On the day of the attack on the World Trade Center, Premier mobilized its listeners to pray for those involved – for the rescuers, the injured, and the bereaved. Many churches were opened for prayer, and Premier collated their details and made them known. Lifeline again had extended hours and was the contact point for information. Premier used its links with churches and ministries in America to find out information, obtain prayer requests and offer support. Many people reported that the Premier website truly gave them the information, inspiration and sense of community which was needed. Only a few years later, the London bombings prompted the need and the response again.

For some people Premier offers worship, teaching and a sense of belonging, but from a church without walls. Premier aims to be a tool for the Church, a resource that complements the services offered by the local church and doesn't compete with it.

It is the same with Lifeline. We are not here to replace pastoral care or the role of the local minister. However, there are many in the wider community who do not feel able to show their face in church, for whatever reason. They may have fallen out with or been offended by friends, family, fellowship, or even God. Churches may have split and people may be hurt and grieving. Their hurt or even pride may be getting in the way of resolving the problems or returning to find fellowship. For these people Premier can be the starting-point of their return. They can listen to worship and teaching without initially having to face 'real' people.

There have been examples when God seems to have engineered people having to face the challenge to return. When Premier first became available on Freeview digital television across the United Kingdom, Lifeline received a telephone call from a person who had been running away from

God and was not attending church, but her television digibox seemed to have a fault – it was stuck on the Premier Freeview channel. Whatever she did, it would seem to return of its own accord. The Lifeline number was displayed on the screen and so she telephoned, recognizing that maybe God was saying something to her. She spoke to one of the team, who led her through a prayer of repentance and reconciliation with God.

Over the years a steady number of people have come to faith through listening to Premier and calling Lifeline. These people have stumbled across Premier's broadcast, or have been given cards or bookmarks with the Lifeline number, or have found one of the websites or activities we have links with – for example, the Rejesus website. Some people with a faith have listened to Premier, as it offers a positive moral way of living, and then have realized that they do not know Jesus as their own personal Lord and Saviour. Just today, as I write this, I have been told of a young person who telephoned at the end of her tether, thinking life was not worth living. The Lifeliner was able to share with her the real meaning of who Jesus is, and his love for her, and then led her in prayer.

Lifeline is not just a telephone helpline but offers responses to emails, which are not restricted to the United Kingdom. People often find it easier to ask questions by email, as this avoids voice-to-voice contact. Deeply personal emails come from within the UK and from many countries overseas. Whether they are struggling with sin, coping with their spouse's adultery, or wanting to find out how to know God for the first time, Lifeline is now serving a broader community than ever anticipated when the vision was conceived. It receives approximately 60,000 calls or emails per year – a total of 630,000 from its launch in 1995 to August 2007. God has enabled Lifeline to offer a service to the Church and its members, wherever they are, and to those outside the Christian community.

Before coming to Premier, I had been a minister. I soon realized that I was seeing more people coming to faith through Premier and Lifeline in a week than I had through the local church in the previous few years. God truly has placed those in the Christian media in a position of great opportunity, and with it, great responsibility to reach out, touch lives, and be there for people at the opportune time for them to meet with God for the first time, or to return to him if they have gone away. It also gives an opportunity for church workers and ministers to find someone to talk to when they would find it impossible to talk within their own church or denomination about doubts, feeling low or stressed, or the need to confess something confidentially.

One of the major achievements of Premier is the bringing together of people and churches to work and share together, thereby creating a real community.

When I started working for Premier and reflected on the changes in the churches in London, I realized the extent to which barriers had been broken down between the churches and the denominations. People were speaking, meeting and working together. Of course, some of this had happened before, but Premier and Lifeline clearly aimed at crossing the boundaries and breaching the barriers. I can now look out at a Premier or Lifeline event and see people from all races, classes, churches and backgrounds sitting next to each other and worshipping together as a family. Within Lifeline I see the same mix of people sitting in our office serving God by answering the telephones.

For our listeners and key stakeholders, there is a wider sense of a Christian community in London and beyond which Premier and Lifeline allow people to feel a part of. In my work I feel privileged to be able to help dispel loneliness and replace it with affirming relationships and a sense of community.

Jonathan Clark

www.premier.org.uk
www.premier.org.uk/lifeline
www.premier.org.uk/response
www.premier.tv
www.rejesus.co.uk
Premier Lifeline: 0845 345 0707. 9 a.m. to midnight daily
Premier Response: 08456 52 52 52. 9 a.m. to 5 p.m. Monday to Friday

Tania Bright

REPRESENTING
THE SERVING
JESUS

Whatever you did for one of the least of these brothers of mine, you did for me.

Matthew 25:40, NIV

Tania Bright worked for two years as SOULINTHECITY LONDON Director of Mobilization, encouraging local churches around the capital to work together in serving their local communities. She now works as a freelance consultant for the Christian sector, and is passionate about representing the serving Jesus.

This is how we know what love is: Jesus Christ laid down his life
for us. And we ought to lay down our lives for our brothers. If anyone
has material possessions and sees his brother in need but has no
pity on him, how can the love of God be in him? Dear children, let
us not love with words or tongue but with actions and in truth.
1 John 3:16–18, NIV

It sounds so easy – let us not love with words or tongue but with actions
and in truth. But experience has shown that it's a challenging exhortation.
There are no simple solutions or formulas that usher in dramatic and
permanent community transformation where the kingdom of heaven floods
every life, home and street. It takes a constant laying down of our lives for
others.

Like me, you may have once innocently thought that Christian 'social
engagement' was straightforward, and all one had to do was unite all the
Christians, pray and 'get out there', doing good works to anyone who we
could do good works to in the name of Jesus! Although my aspirations
were admirable, I needed realism and spiritual sensitivity in order to discern
how to engage and *when* – and to listen to God to find strategies so that
the community transformation journey was the 'long race' and not the
'short sprint'.

I now find myself some years into being committed to community
regeneration – still believing, passionately, in a God who can transform, yet
feeling a little overwhelmed by the 'long race'. I see all around me complex,
multi-layered dimensions of community breakdown and fragmentation, and
I stop and wonder, just wonder how we can offer genuine, long-lasting
solutions to the pain we see around us, in the name of Jesus?

The encouragement is that transformation has taken place before. We
have seen pockets of revival through history where the Holy Spirit grabs a
community or town and metamorphoses the social and spiritual

infrastructures. Amazing and Herculean changes take place. These examples of renewal are sweet, spirit-warming elixirs to the believer who cannot see in the natural realm how on earth crippling personal debt can be tackled, life-controlling addictions can be curbed, families can be restored, baby-fathers can become role-models, the elderly can be affirmed and respected once more, and our youth can learn to live together, not killing each other over postcodes.

So we know, and still trust, that it is God's desire and intent to renew and restore his communities, towns, villages, cities – nationally and globally. But what is our role in this? As Andy Frost has written in his earlier section of this book, when we *represent* Jesus and his kingdom values, we begin to find solutions to the world's problems. We also then gain an opportunity to *present* who Jesus really is to a world that is ready to listen.

But how do we represent Jesus in today's post-modern culture? One quick scan across the Christian horizon will tell us that there are many forms and many methodologies. Social action or social engagement is one such way forward to represent the values of Christ in our communities through serving, assisting, caring and volunteering – all with the aim of being a blessing to humanity, God's most prized creation. The minute we begin serving those around us, as soon as trust is built, the moment we genuinely relationally connect with people – we create natural and appropriate ways to *present* Jesus to people who have begun to listen.

There is no doubt that across the country there are Christians who are pouring themselves into their communities in the name of Jesus, and one chapter alone would never be enough to name and recognize the churches, projects, leaders and individuals at the heart of what God is doing. We can, however, take valuable lessons from one major social action initiative outlined below.

In 2004 a two-week Christian social action initiative called SOULINTHECITY LONDON mobilized over 20,000 Christian young people and 750 churches, who, motivated by their faith in Jesus Christ, swamped the streets of London, engaging in over 600 community projects. Tony Blair, the then Prime Minister, said of it: 'SOULINTHECITY is an immensely worthwhile venture. I am delighted to give it my support.'

Over three years on, there is still a ripple effect of this 'worthwhile' initiative happening across the capital, because people saw something of the divine happen in the day-to-day through serving our community selflessly and passionately. Churches across London are still continuing the legacy of SOULINTHECITY LONDON by building on what they started in 2004.

The local church

One town in west London ran firm and fast with the two-week initiative in 2004, running 26 projects, involving over 1,500 delegates and volunteers from across 15 different churches in the area. All the main-line denominations were involved, including Pioneer churches, Free Evangelical churches, and the Salvation Army. All the projects were born out of the local churches finding a need in their particular parish or area and bringing these ideas to the collective table to discuss them. There was a great cross-selection of 'social action' planned for the two weeks in the summer: Fun-Days, BBQs, painting murals on the key estates, cleaning filthy stairwells in council blocks, planting community gardens, urban dance workshops for 'yoof', day-trips for the elderly to Kew Gardens – to name just a few of the activities.

The local authorities

Virtually all these activities had to be covered by local authority permission at one level or another. At first this seemed hard work and layered with red tape, but the more the projects were discussed, the more the council realized that the local churches genuinely wanted to make a difference in their community, and doors were flung open. Comments were made by the council such as, 'We've never been offered this level of volunteerism before from within the community, and the last place we expected it from was the Church!' Christians were stepping out of the four walls of their church buildings, taking ownership and presenting themselves professionally. The end result was that the credibility of the local churches sky-rocketed. It was realized that the Church could actually 'deliver' something, that it was not an outdated institution that hid behind a religious façade. Whilst there were and continue to be what seem like bureaucratic, time-wasting application processes in working with local authorities, a level of understanding was reached in which the churches and the council supported each other's agendas and ultimately ensured safety and professionalism for the community. But most importantly, lessons were learnt about the fact that by working together – the Church, the council, the voluntary groups, the local businesses – more can be achieved.

There were the occasional difficult conversations with Departmental Heads, where they would ask questions such as, 'Are you trying to convert people to your faith by doing these projects?' and 'Are you prepared to work with people of other faiths?' Matt Bird, the then SOULINTHECITY LONDON Public Affairs Director, came up with a response which often diffused possible tension in trying to answer with honesty, stating, 'We're faith-based, not faith biased.' Often there was then a chance to talk candidly about the Christian faith, and to explain that it was precisely that faith that motivated the local churches to want to serve their community.

Who paid?

Finance was not something that proved too much of a challenge for these churches in west London, as a few of the key churches were incredibly generous. They gave large amounts of money to be used for the greater good of London, not just for projects within a quarter-mile radius of their church! Coming together as a team was a humbling and steep learning curve for the local churches. If those generous local churches had not been so sacrificial in their giving, a significant number of the projects that ran might not have been possible.

This does beg the question of how to set up social action projects in areas where the local churches may not have the financial or practical resources to invest in the local community. To help such churches, an extensive list of available resources has been gathered in an appendix at the end of this book. And on a spiritual level, a useful (but slightly simplistic) saying is: 'If it's God's will, it's God's bill!'

God's provision

In 2004, the local authority did contribute token amounts for paint, gardening material and refreshments for volunteers, all of which was gratefully received. The bigger miracle was that in the years *after* 2004 – after the Church had shown its love, compassion, skills, effort, capacity for caring and agenda-free motivation – over £40,000 was offered to SOULINTHECITY LONDON projects in this one town alone by the local authorities.

Honour the people already on the ground

In devising the 2004 projects, it was realized that many people, of many faiths and of none, were already working hard at bringing about positive change in the community. These people needed to be honoured and listened to, and most of all learnt from. In all the pre-project research, people from Tenants' Associations, caretakers of estates, youth workers, and local councillors were actively sought out. Through listening hard, the local churches really 'got' what was troubling residents in the area, and understood how they could help physically, practically and spiritually. If the SOULINTHECITY LONDON projects had not in any way worked alongside the local institutions, then we would have been in jeopardy of simply doing things to people and places that we thought were a good idea.

> *'Poor' people often feel that 'do-gooders' who have not lived in their situation, parachute in and set up projects to help them without even involving them or talking to them. If we do not engage with people in poverty before 'doing' something to help, we are assuming that we know what they need and that we are the 'experts' of their lives. We will act like 'benefactors' to the lowly poor rather than partners in their struggle. Such attitudes in our social action create and sustain imbalances of power, and keep the poor dependent on the 'benefactor' rather than empowering them to be in control of their lives. They cut across the attitude of servanthood that Jesus talked about and modelled. In our attempts to make a difference, we must always ask ourselves the question 'Are we doing things to people, for people or with people?'*
> From the *Shaftesbury Social Action Guides*

Inspirational unity

The unity displayed through churches working together, regardless of doctrinal and denominational differences, was a beautiful expression of God's kingdom. What *could* be done together was focused on, rather than what *couldn't*. When the Church is in this place, it's a powerful force to be reckoned with. It once again has a voice that speaks out of unity and wisdom. Not everything had to be 'perfect', only strong enough for a platform to be built that allowed Christians to positively speak into what we're *for*, rather than what we're *against*, and for it to sound compassionate and articulate to the community around us.

Steps forward

For a few years after 2004, the local churches still continued working with the local authority and delivered creative social action projects in the area. The yearly high-points were the Family Fun days in local parks, bringing all the community together to enjoy free food and activities, yet creating an environment where people could be prayed for and receive invites to Alpha groups and local church services. Significantly, however, one of the key requests that members of local churches would get from those in the community was, 'Do you know where I can go for debt advice? We're struggling!'

It transpired that there was nowhere in this suburban town for people to go for financial help, since the Citizens Advice Bureau had shut down years before. The churches really sought God on this, and decided that this was where their key focus should be. After much research and investigation into Christian debt organizations, a company called Christians Against Poverty (CAP) was contacted, and a partnership was formed. Running a Debt Centre has now become one of the primary ways in which these local churches serve their community. It is financially run by donations from individuals and the local churches, and has assisted and continues to assist many people out of debt and into financial freedom, whilst at the same time offering the clients an opportunity to be prayed with and to invite God into their lives and worlds. There was a realization that sometimes partnerships and agencies can be the answer in delivering long-term sustainable community engagement. The local church doesn't always have to think of itself as the sole provider. Through this partnership, the local congregations have been able to utilize CAP's expertise and business acumen.

So through this example – one of many – we can see an inspiring example of local churches working together to engage with society in a real and transforming way. Some key aspects to be drawn out are: tailoring the projects to the local community; working with local authorities; partnering with local churches; and creating sustainable projects that can continue to impact communities in the long term.

Most importantly, let our core motivation for community transformation be an act of faith, to represent Jesus to those who so desperately need him. Whether or not this brings the Church growth, attention or fast results, let this remain at the heart of all we do. Then, when God breaks through, we're there – ready, poised, in the thick of it, relationally connected, trusted – able to *present* Jesus to people whose hearts are ready.

> *I was hungry and you fed me,*
> *I was thirsty and you gave me a drink,*
> *I was homeless and you gave me a room,*
> *I was shivering and you gave me clothes,*
> *I was sick and you stopped to visit,*
> *I was in prison and you came to me.*
>
> Based on Matthew 25:35–36

Tania Bright
www.hope08.com
www.faithworks.info
www.shaftesburysociety.org

Jonathan Olyode

REPRESENTING
THE PRAYING
JESUS

But Jesus often withdrew to lonely places and prayed.

Luke 5:16, NIV

Jonathan Oloyede is on the senior leadership team of Glory House Church as their Community Director. He also leads the UK response to the Global Day of Prayer, which is a key part of the Pentecost Festival. He wants to mobilize the Church in the UK to more effectively represent the praying Jesus.

French fries or Jewish falafel?

In the blazing heat of the Middle East, with temperatures well over thirty degrees, we travelled up a winding, dusty road leading to Mount Carmel, south of Haifa city. The year was 2000 and it was my third trip to Israel as the team leader of a group of about thirty students from the Glory House Bible School, of which I was Principal. We arrived at the foot of the mountain feeling very thirsty and dehydrated. After some cool drinks and local falafel (a Jewish delicacy), we were driven to the top of the mountain in old Mercedes Benz cars nicknamed 'Camels'. Mount Carmel stood in full glory with lush valleys all around. This stop was part of our tour and I wanted to maximize the moment by reliving the classic biblical encounter between Elijah and the prophets of Baal.

Incidentally, as we made the journey, our Israeli Zionist guide, Ami, and the driver of our tour bus, Benjamin, told us of the severe weather conditions in Israel. At that time it had not rained in several months. Agricultural conditions were getting critical. I responded by crazily declaring that we would pray for rain. As I stood in the blazing heat and looked up to the clear blue sky, not a cloud in sight, I thought it may not have been a good idea after all!

My team consisted of a number of African and Caribbean brothers and sisters from various churches across London, most of whom were Pentecostal by tradition. It was therefore easy to get them praying 'in the Spirit' and in tongues when we arrived at the top of Mount Carmel. We prayed out loud for about fifteen minutes.

Shortly after our prayer session, a group of tourists of various nationalities walked up to us and specifically asked to know who amongst us was from Haiti. My assistant Cynthia replied that we were all from London and none of us was Haitian. They were quite emphatic and insisted that one of us must be from Haiti because they had heard that person speaking and praying the Haitian language! We tried explaining that we were praying in tongues and that we were all Pentecostal Christians from London.

No sooner had we returned to the bus, thinking that was quite a miracle, when Ami walked up to me with a strange look on his face. He had been in some sort of heated debate with Benjamin the driver. He asked Francis, a francophone Congolese student who struggled with English, where he had learnt to speak fluent Hebrew. In an excited tone, Ami went on to further explain that Francis' Hebrew was of the calibre spoken by his great uncle. I explained that Francis was from Congo and barely spoke English, and without any doubt did not speak Hebrew at all! Apparently, while Francis was praying in tongues, Benjamin was hearing Hebrew! Seizing the moment, I opened the Bible to the second chapter of Acts and began to share the Gospel with Ami, explaining what he had just experienced. I introduced him to Jesus that day and prayed with him to become a Christian. Two weeks later he sent me a very appreciative email thanking us for his daughter, who had been miraculously healed during our visit. He also finished with a footnote stating that it had been raining cats and dogs in Tel-Aviv and all over Israel since we left!

The power tool

Prayer is powerful. Prayer is real. Prayer is relevant. Prayer works wonders. Prayer combined with fasting can produce tremendous results. At the time of writing this, a protégé of mine called me in great distress because his fiancée had been rushed to hospital in deep pain caused by stomach ulcers. I was fasting at the time and I prayed with him fervently on the phone. I told him to go and lay his hands on her and declare the simple words, 'By the stripes of Jesus you are healed' (see Isa. 53:5). She was completely healed through the power of prayer and was in church that same night, jumping around and serving God like nothing had happened.

The Church was birthed in prayer. The Scriptures say in Acts 1:14 (NIV), 'They all joined together constantly in prayer, along with the women and Mary the mother of Jesus, and with his brothers.' On the day of Pentecost the power of God fell on a prayer meeting, releasing power through the Holy Spirit. Peter's sermon on that same day resulted in 3,000 being baptized into Christ!

One might ask, 'Is there truly a divine Power that overrules the destinies of nations? Can this power be effectively invoked by prayer with fasting?' 2 Chronicles 20:1–30 gives a very striking account of God's intervention in the lives of his people. Realizing that he had no military resources with which to meet the enemy's challenge, Jehoshaphat turned to God for help. God's people were called to unite in public collective fasting and prayer for divine intervention. Men, women and children were all included. Through a prophetic utterance from a Levite, the Holy Spirit gave direction, assurance and encouragement. The outcome of the saga was that there was no need for Judah to use any kind of military weapon because the entire army of the enemy destroyed themselves!

A lesson to be learnt from this account is the fact that spiritual power has supremacy over natural power (2 Cor. 10:4). Collective fasting, united prayer, the supernatural gifts of the Holy Spirit and public praise were the powerful spiritual weapons employed by the people of Judah. These weapons, if employed by Christians today, will culminate in victories as powerful and dramatic as those experienced by God's people in the days of Jehoshaphat.

The book of Acts is riddled with people in prayer. Chapter 3 begins with Peter and John going to the temple 'at the hour of prayer', and as a result a crippled man was completely healed. When the leaders were threatened in the next chapter, they came together and prayed for boldness. In response the Holy Ghost physically shook the meeting place and filled them again.

A careful study of the early Church reveals three repetitive keys to the secret of their powerful ministry: corporate unity, prayer with fasting, and preaching the Gospel. The very essence of Pentecost is power and grace from heaven coming down upon ordinary people for the witness and preaching of the Gospel. The Church is waking up to the key and power of prayer.

I was invited to speak at a Soul Survivor youth camp in Somerset, England. My session was being conducted under a tent, and the rain was belting down while I spoke. I shouted into the microphone: 'Rain, I command you to stop now' – and right on cue, it stopped instantly.

During another session with the young people, I was teaching on the power of Pentecost, the Holy Spirit, and the laying on of hands. I told the boys and girls to lay hands on and pray for everyone who was ill. After they had prayed for a few minutes, I stopped them and asked them what had happened. The whole place exploded with testimonies of the power of God.

A tall young man near the entrance was jumping up so high and for so long that I thought he would hurt himself. He had come into the meeting walking on crutches and had been in great pain the day before. His leg and ankle were completely healed, right on the spot, as hands were laid on him.

This challenge goes out to you, the reader: *Begin to do this in faith and in prayer.* The Bible says, 'they will place their hands on sick people, and they will get well' (Mark 16:18, NIV). These signs and this power are available to all Christians who will just believe.

Drop your agenda

As a young man in medical school, I was a very devout Muslim and was constantly searching for the meaning of life. I used to pray five times a day and would always beseech Allah to speak to me, which he never did. I gave my life to Christ in a prayer meeting led by a bunch of students on my university campus.

I had a very interesting dream that same day, in which our hostel was suddenly ablaze with flames, and in order to escape the flames we all ran onto the roof, with the closest safe rooftop over forty feet away. I heard a voice say to me, 'Jump!' But I replied, 'No human being can jump that distance and survive.' The voice authoritatively told me again, 'Jump!' Like Neo in *The Matrix*, I jumped and landed safely on the other side. I turned to see my friends almost engulfed in the flames, and the voice said to me, 'Begin to pray for your friends' – and then I woke up. I obeyed that instruction and began to minister to my colleagues. I laid hands on them and saw incredible healings and deliverances.

Shortly after medical school I came to the UK in 1991 and within days of arriving, God said to me:

You are not here by accident but by divine design as part of my recruitment to this part of the world in preparation for the coming of my Son, Jesus. So drop your agenda and pick up my programme.

I had incredible visions given to me by God concerning the United Kingdom. I will elaborate on these visions later, but I saw what looked like a national day of prayer where all Christian leaders and people from all denominations came together to worship and praise God. I also saw visions of young people – multitudes of them coming out of banks, schools, homes, colleges, off the streets, everywhere! God was revealing to me that the young people are going to be very active in his move over this nation.

Wake up Britain!

When I came to this country, I was taken aback and shocked by the spiritual state of the nation. Everywhere I looked, there was a great decay of Christianity and its values. This great missionary-sending nation was in a terrible state. I was ignorant and naive, thinking most Britons were church-goers!

Even though the spiritual fabric of our beloved nation is in tatters, I strongly believe the Church can turn the tide through fasting and prayer. Intense, quiet or loud, but always heartfelt, prayer is the master key to opening a fresh climate over the UK. Many private altars are dry and desolate. They need to be re-visited with tears of repentance and intercession. God is looking for vessels to use. He needs us because without a yielded heart he can do very little.

I believe with all of my heart that as the Church rediscovers unity, prayer and preaching the Gospel, we will see the power of God and the love of Christ spread throughout the whole nation. That is why I got involved with SOULINTHECITY and why we have stepped out in faith to champion the Global Day of Prayer across the city of London and the rest of the nation.

If you've read this far, I want to humbly challenge you to go back to your closet, to increase your frequency and intensity in everyday prayer and communion with the Lord. Many of us are praying but we need to pray *more!*

If my people, who are called by my name, will humble themselves and pray and seek my face and turn from their wicked ways, then will I hear from heaven and will forgive their sin and will heal their land.

2 Chronicles 7:14, NIV

The Global Day of Prayer

If you are sensitive to trends in the Church and in the Spirit, you will recognize that there is a call to prayer coming upon the global Church. New forms of churches are emerging as towns, cities and villages all over the whole world are experiencing fresh expressions of Christianity. One such clear sign is the Global Day of Prayer, which started in South Africa just after the turn of the new millennium. By 2007 an estimated half a billion

Christians across the globe in over 200 countries were joined together in repentance and prayer on Pentecost Sunday.

In the United Kingdom we have joined in this upsurge of united prayer. Around 20,000 Christians came together at West Ham Stadium to pray at the second Global Day of Prayer in London. By 2012, it is hoped that the Church in this nation will have established major prayer chains, events and initiatives all over the country that will usher in Christ-centred missions and acts of mercy. The afterglow of these will bring transformation to our local neighbourhoods, estates, schools and communities.

London's Global Day of Prayer chapter started in February 2006 when a group of leaders from London and across the nation met at Holy Trinity Brompton to listen to the vision(s) that God had given me for united prayer across the capital and the British Isles. To help you understand the prayer movement emerging from London, I will elaborate on three visions given to me.

Visions, dreams, trances and prophetic revelations are all biblical and can be experienced by any Christian as a result of gifts by the Holy Spirit, or as chosen by the Lord. Peter quoted from the book of Joel on the day of Pentecost when he said:

> *In the last days, God says, 'I will pour out my Spirit on all people. Your sons and daughters will prophesy, your young men will see visions, your old men will dream dreams. Even on my servants, both men and women, I will pour out my Spirit in those days, and they will prophesy.'*
>
> Acts 2:17–18, NIV

God has spoken to me many times through dreams and visions, right from the day when I encountered Jesus as my Saviour. With this in mind, let me now tell you what I saw.

The road to Wembley

The first vision showed thousands of people who looked like Christians worshipping and praying at Wembley stadium. At that time, 1992, I had never been to the stadium but had seen it on TV. However, the stadium I saw was more modern than the Wembley stadium I knew. It was a different stadium, but in the experience I just knew that it was definitely Wembley.

Everybody was there to celebrate and pray. The large podium was all set and ready, but empty. We all seemed to be waiting for someone to come to speak. Lots of Christian leaders and speakers were there, but all of them were stationary and looking at the microphone. As I looked on and waited, the Lord said to my heart:

> Jonathan, when my people gather in unity, I am the one who speaks. When two or three gather together in my name, there I am in the midst of them.

I recorded the vision in my heart and rehearsed it to a number of leaders. I didn't know what was required of me, so I prayed for unity in the Body of Christ and later shelved the vision. Nevertheless I did not forget it.

The Pied Piper

The second vision I experienced concerning the UK came to me around 1997. I saw hundreds of thousands of people, probably over a million, streaming out from nightclubs, libraries, homes, streets, pubs, workplaces, factories, churches, mosques, temples, city centres . . . everywhere. Some were well dressed, others looked like they were homeless. Their hairstyles were of all shapes, shades and styles. The striking thing was that they were all *teenagers*.

It looked like a scene from the Pied Piper fable, with a Stephen King eerie twist, as they all seemed to be responding to a certain call or sound. They had a dreamy look on their faces, but their foreheads were ridged with determination and purpose. They were teenagers from all cultural groups and nationalities, but the overwhelming majority were Caucasian Brits. They poured onto the empty streets and filled the dual carriageway as far as my eyes could see. It looked like the M1.

I came out of the dream or vision shouting in my mind, 'They are here! They are all here!!' I suddenly *knew* that Britain was a Christian nation, and I heard the Lord say, 'When I call, My sheep hear My voice, respond and obey.'

The vision that I saw, where thousands or perhaps a million young Britons were responding to God, is in sharp contrast with this present hedonistic, self-serving and liberal society. As a British-born Nigerian, saved from Islam and called as a missionary to Great Britain, I see a Western world that has travelled far from its Judeo-Christian foundations.

The third reel

The Lord gave me a simple illustration about *joining the dots*. I saw what looked like a map of the British Isles with the locations of all the churches – in homes, factories, shops, historic buildings or converted warehouses. They were linked together.

Each church was praying the same prayer as the next, and there was some cord or connection joining each church with the others. I clearly saw each church as groups of people or congregations praying together. I can best describe their numbers as fives, fifties, five hundreds and five thousands. On top of each gathering was a lightbulb or a flame of fire. Then, as the people continued to pray, all the churches lit up as individual lights, and it seemed that the whole country was covered in neon glory like a Christmas tree!

I saw the words 'LIGHT' and 'HEALING' emblazoned across the map of the United Kingdom. I noted that each group was not necessarily a formal church or denomination but Christians joined together in prayer. It seemed to me that wherever Christians were gathered to pray for God's kingdom to come, heaven recognized their meeting. I strongly believe that when the Church begins to pray in unity, divine light and healing will come to the British Isles like a tidal wave.

The call

One of the key legacies I have inherited from my sojourn in Islam is a discipline and devotion to prayer. I truly believe with all my heart that if Christians began to take prayer more seriously, this nation would be changed. God is calling you to intensify your prayer life and repair your private altar if it is dry and desolate. Repent of your busyness and begin to pull away into quietness. You and I need to spend and 'waste' time in God's presence. We need to listen more than we talk. We need to wait for his instructions before acting. Faith must precede intelligence. Stillness must be a step ahead of strategy.

God is calling his Church back into the Sabbath rest where we lay down all our burdens, and rest. In this day and age, the greatest warfare against the Christian is the battle to be still and quiet in God's presence. Be still so that you can know God. Knowing God is your strength, your muscles and your armour. My encouragement to you, dear reader, is to fight the good fight of rest. Fight to find the time. Wrestle with your schedule, your diary, your e-mails, your mobile phone, your TV and your flesh. Fight your way into Psalm 23:2. Beat the path into his presence, where weights disappear and burdens melt (Matt. 11:28–30).

Knowing God and making him known can only come from the knowledge of his presence.

Jonathan Oloyede
www.gloryhouse.org.uk
www.gdoplondon.com

THE CHURCH AS JESUS
Kit Lewis

Now you are the body of Christ, and each one of you is a part of it.

1 Corinthians 12:27, NIV

Kit Lewis is the Project Manager for the Pentecost Festival. After eighteen months of grappling with these issues, he is still fascinated by the idea that the sole body on earth that Jesus appointed to continue his ministry, is the Church.

The Church does a lot. This book fails to and, of course, was never able to represent *all* that the Church is doing. With so many differing Christian denominations, agencies, charities, groups and individuals, it is simply impossible to write about – or indeed, to present through a single weekend festival – the *complete* Church. And yet, all of the examples of the active Church in this book, and hundreds more besides, are being profiled in some way at the Pentecost Festival 2008. It stands as a Festival that showcases the Church.

Quality, warts and all

I was terrified.

Of course, I was hugely excited by the challenge of project managing such a Festival. Yes, I was thrilled to be working with such a great team. And yes, I admit it, I was scared that we might not get anywhere near the huge vision with such minimal funding and little experience of events on this scale in London. But when Rob and Andy Frost first shared the vision of the Pentecost Festival with me, my overriding fear was much more than this. I was scared for the Church.

Let me explain.

The Pentecost Festival has two primary aims:

1. To resource – to inspire and encourage groups, agencies, churches and individuals alike, as they experience and contribute to the melting-pot of expression, culture and style that is the breadth of the living Church; and to introduce developments, new concepts and approaches, and best practices to the people of the Church.

And, more fundamentally:

2. To represent – to showcase the spread of work, to promote the diversity of engagement and to highlight the plethora of Christian agencies, charities, groups and individuals that are impacting and transforming the world as Church.

Great aims, a brilliant idea and a massive vision – so what was there to fear? Surely excitement should overpower fear in situations like this. But something that I was not expecting was holding me back.

Put simply, I was scared that the Church would look foolish trying to compete with society. Scared that the Church's music, theatre, comedy, political engagement, charitable work, sport and whatever else would look somewhat pale and pallid, amateurish and shoddy, against those of the world's entertainment industries and events.

The vision for the Pentecost Festival is to showcase the breadth of the Church. Part of me wants the Festival to work as a foundation from which the Church can parade its true colours, stand up and say, 'Look at this, look at what we do.' But another part of me wants the Church to keep quiet for fear of it being mocked. Will these events look slapdash and small-time in London, one of the leading world cities?

If we are to flaunt the Festival as 'The best the Church has to offer', or with some other hyperbolic tag-line, it will have the nation's media watching carefully. Part of me thought that encouraging the Church – local, national and international – to bring events to London was putting the institution of Christianity in the stocks of publicity and inviting the national press to throw the tomatoes and sponges of ridicule. And throw them right in its face. Very hard.

A capital city that leads the way in entertainment, economics, politics, sports and events surely overpowers, overshadows and overawes the work of an obsolete, uninteresting, religious body.

Or does it?

During the Festival's development we held countless meetings and discussion groups, looking at booking procedures and how smaller events might work over the weekend. One particular time Rob, Andy, a couple of friends and I sat down to think about how we might work some quality control into the events. Surely, for the Pentecost Festival to be successful, it needed to have a commitment to excellence and look good.

I am sure you have met that crazy lady from the local Methodist church who makes jam from her surplus rhubarb and distributes it at traffic lights to passing strangers. She does it as an example of our responsibility to local farming and the generosity of God. We could not possibly have her involved in the Festival. Imagine if the *Metro* or some other newspaper got hold of that! It is not credible and it is not excellent. There would be egg on the lady's face, on the Festival's face and, more worryingly, on the face of the Church.

'I guess we could audition them all,' I suggested. But if there were to be over 200 events going on over the Saturday daytime alone, this would become a logistical nightmare, nor would this encourage confidence in groups and churches. 'Or we could allow only those we invited,' I continued. We could easily identify groups and organizations that would be well suited to getting involved, and recruit only their support.

Time and time again, in this meeting as in so many others, we were reminded of Rob's initial premise: *a festival that Jesus would want to come to.* 'How would Jesus keep out the dross?' I thought.

'Failing that, we could just have something like "We have the right to reject any application" in the small print, and then decide their suitability from their given description, past events, and profile,' was my final offer. Of course, we would not know how good the event was going to be until the day, nor would we be able to stop a contribution to the Festival after it had begun, but we would be keeping some kind of editorial control over content.

'How would Jesus keep control?' we wondered.

Eventually we realized that Jesus would not have kept control. Nor would he have tried to keep people out. Jesus was open to everybody, and anyone who believed in him was welcomed as a follower. This is an example and a challenge for the Church. I was happy to include everybody in this Festival as long as they were credible. This is not genuine inclusion.

The Church now, just like Jesus' followers then, is all who believe, whatever they are engaged in and whatever they do – from tax collectors to tent makers, from fishermen to sellers of purple.

With this in mind, and if we wanted to be true to our vision to 'represent the breadth of the Church', how could we tell a group or individual that what they did had no place here? 'I'm sorry, my dear, but God does not approve of your Toddler Ice-cream Olympics training course. . . . I don't care how many lives you've changed or hearts you've transformed through it. . . . No, it's just not Church.'

The truth is that it *is* Church. If an individual or group can sign a declaration of faith in Jesus, then they are Church. And it is right to represent the *true* breadth of the Church's work. Ice-cream Olympics? You're in. Edith and her rhubarb jam? You're in. From street dancers to scientists, from musicians to sportsmen, from skate-boarders to bread-makers, they are Church. Let us celebrate all that the Church does in London and around the country. There is no reason to fear the involvement of the unknown. If you are committed to the teaching of Jesus, come and stand with us. Let us not be ashamed of the Gospel, nor of the Gospel's representation on earth – the Church. Let us showcase the whole Church, warts and all.

The Church does a lot. And I am proud of it.

Quantity and variety

The Church is not dead.

The Pentecost Festival is meant to prompt the same reaction from everyone – from bishops and builders, from ministers and mime artists, from church-goers and society at large: 'I didn't know that the Church was *all of this*!'

Everyone knows something about the Church – old buildings, *Songs of Praise*, Sunday morning services, weddings, funerals, a homeless shelter, a youth group. And some know more than others – books of the Bible in order, the latest national initiative, the name and date of the next new festival. But none of us know everything about it.

Ten high-quality, large events put on by some of the biggest charities in the world in brilliant London venues cannot begin to represent the Church's activity in the UK, and its commitment to the world. Christian Aid's swing dance in Waterloo; Authentic Media's gig at the Astoria on Tottenham Court Road; Release International's focus on Indian and Bollywood culture at Westminster Central Hall; Survivor's worship-gig; Open Doors' and Saltmine's music competition, 'Hope Academy'; CARE's MP panel discussion on faith and culture; Compassion's focus on child poverty around the world; Bible Society's presentation of the *Luv Esther* musical; Christian In Science's and Faraday Institute's look at the interface between faith and science; and Emerging Culture's comedy and club night at the Soho Revue Bar – all these events show something of the remarkable wealth of the Church's engagement, but they do not represent the Church totally.

A few months into the Pentecost Festival project management role, and I felt pretty happy talking with organizations and individuals about the Festival and its developments. I enjoy talking and, to be honest, getting people excited about the Festival was pretty easy. International charities, high-profile venues, big-name speakers and the best of UK Christian music is not a difficult collection to sell. And I felt comfortable doing exactly this – selling the concept as the breadth of the Church and the content as the best of the Christian world. In fact, the reaction I had become accustomed to receiving began with a general air of admiration for the concept and was followed by a discussion on how they might involve themselves in the weekend.

I was sat in the office of the director of a faith charity whose primary foci are community and local church. I started the big sell: 'showcasing what the Church is all about – it's more than *Songs of Praise*'; 'we're creating a platform from which the Church can speak credibly'; 'in society, for society'; 'the groups, venues and names already involved include. . . .' He sat and he listened patiently, he nodded and he smiled when I reeled off the contributors.

I sat back and awaited the queries as to how he might involve his organization. They did not come. Instead, we became engaged in a conversation about exactly how these high-profile organizations represented the breadth of the Church. I put forward the stock argument of a spread of diversity in social engagement and the size of the groups involved, feeling fairly confident that this would prove that we are depicting a true spread of Church and put this guy in his place.

It did not. Actually, his response was more piercing and more challenging than I ever suspected. He was not bowled over by the glitz of the Big 10, nor by my continued assurance that it would be the kind of Festival Jesus would want to go to. He asked, quite simply, 'How does this show the *local* church?'

It was in this little office in central London that it struck me, quite clearly. Jesus would not want to come to an event that had superstars as its primary draw. But more than this, Jesus would only come to an event that not only championed those who serve the Church, but also displayed the everyday community church engagement. The Festival must not ask local churches and groups to do something for it, using their resources of time and money to enhance the Festival; rather, it must identify what churches and groups already do and show it off. The Festival has to say, 'Your work is impressive', and ask, 'Please can we showcase it?' It's a simple but important shift; ask not what you can do for the Festival, but what the Festival can do for you. The Festival now serves the individuals, the groups, the churches and the organizations – they do not serve it.

Adding to the Big 10 two hundred smaller-scale public events and a massive stadium finale goes some way towards beginning to unpack the thousands upon thousands of specific projects, practices and pastimes with which the different members of the Church engage. Yet the result still falls short in an attempt to exhibit the remarkable spread of what the Church is doing. It showcases much of the Church, but by no means all. Likewise, the preceding chapters in this book speak of a tiny fraction of the work with which a tiny fraction of the participants in the Pentecost Festival engage – a Festival that is itself a tiny fragment of the Church at work in the UK.

It is this fraction of the Church's work that I have had the privilege of helping facilitate into an easily accessible weekend heap of events. But this heap makes up a Festival more vibrant and bright, more public and accessible, more diverse and with more contributors than I have ever seen. True, I am only 25 years old, but the older Christians whom I have quizzed have all been unable to name a single event in the Christian calendar with such a high-profile line-up of arts and sports, such a mix of cultures and ages, such varied political and spiritual themes, such strength of academia and spiritual renewal. It is remarkable to see so much of the Church in society, for society.

The Church is all of these things and incontrovertibly more. The Church does a lot.

Upper room and marketplace

The accounts of that first Pentecost are sensational and bizarre.

We read about an inspirational and passionate leader of a revolutionary movement who is murdered and seemingly defeated. His followers meet together in secret and – as we are all prone to do in times of despair – they pray. When there is nothing else that can be done, when all seems lost and there is no solution, it is a natural human reaction to cry out for help. They pray and they stand terrified as, out of nowhere, a surge of power surrounds and pulses through them. It is as though the heart and influence of their leader is in this room on the second floor. And with this presence strange things happen, their confidence grows, and they begin to understand this situation.

He lived with them, he challenged them, he inspired them and finally he died for them. But this was not the finale; he sent his Spirit to stay with them – to inspire, encourage and develop them into an active, passionate people who speak truth, challenge injustice and love remarkably. Today we often dumb down or reduce quite how fundamental the Holy Spirit is for the continuation of Jesus' revolutionary movement. People get scared talking about the spiritual. But prayer and the Spirit are central.

Pentecost People is the spiritual hub of the Pentecost Festival weekend, providing a place and some time for people to gather and pray. The final aspect of the Festival is the Global Day of Prayer, where tens of thousands gather to pray for each other, local communities and the world. These two features of the Festival provide times to connect with God, encourage faith and re-invite his Spirit – a kind of resource for the soul. It's daring and terrifying to suggest a recreation of the disciples' experience in that upper room shortly after their leader left. It's a daring but compelling suggestion. . . .

And what happened to the group when they became invigorated, inspired and sustained by the Holy Spirit? They connected with people. They moved from a place of introspective fear to visible engagement. They moved from the upper room to the marketplace. This was no longer a group of broken, timid people looking back to how things were with the support of their leader, but a revolutionary movement of men and women committed to communicating their life, lifestyle and life-sustaining God with the world.

With Pentecost People and the Global Day of Prayer, people are being challenged to be part of this Spirit-led revolution to communicate faith and life in understandable terms. Just as the disciples spoke in different languages to tell their message, the Pentecost Festival communicates through a variety of ways. The weekend's Festival Feel – all day on Saturday

– attempts to communicate life and God through hip-hop, street dance, clowning, scientific discussion, sport, fine art, food and much more. It is through these that the message of this 2,000-year-old revolutionary movement is spoken.

And the name of this revolutionary movement? We call it Church.

What does the Church represent?

A question that I've been considering for well over a year is, 'What sort of Festival would Jesus want to go to?' Perhaps a more suitable question, and a relevant one, considering our discussion about Church, is 'What sort of Church would Jesus want to go to?'

I am frustrated with Church.

I am not frustrated with Church content. I sing, I pray, I meet with God, I talk, and then I leave. It's a nice hour, it's an hour of learning and sometimes it can be a powerful life-enhancing hour or so. But that's just it – it is an hour. I do it, and then leave it. Now, if I add to that a study group and a weekly evening of youth work, it looks more like four or five hours a week of Church. What really frustrates me about this is that I can put a time-frame on what I do as Church.

This is not the example that I read in the New Testament. If I look at Jesus' example and the initial experiences of his disciples after he left, I come up with a few answers pointing towards what Church is actually all about.

The first thing I notice is that Church is not in any one place. It has been said time and time again that Church is not the building but the people. The Church is personal – a personal response to the Holy Spirit often expressed in a group who share this same motivation. Church is always action in response to the Holy Spirit.

The second thing I notice is that Church does not stop. We are not called to 'go to' Church, or to 'do' Church, but to 'be' Church, and to be

Church all day every day. It is not a service but a lifestyle; it is not an event but a personal mission. Yes, there are key points in the collective's response to the Holy Spirit – the Sunday service, the weekly coffee morning, the annual festivals – but to be Church we have to act justly and pray without ceasing 24 hours a day, 365 days a year. Neither Jesus nor the disciples could turn their mission off.

So in search of what Church is, I find myself focused on people, on lifestyles and on Spirit-leading. The question is no longer 'What sort of Church would Jesus want to go to?' but rather 'What sort of life would Jesus lead?' It is the responsibility of every single member of every single church in every single village, town or city to represent the mission of this revolutionary movement.

It really does start with you, your heart and your commitment to the mission. I am sure you, the reader, are agreeing with this. I have said nothing controversial, revelatory, or new. But this book is not about new things. It is about now-things. Today children are dying, people are suffering, and the mission of the Church – of your church – remains incomplete. This book is not simply a pat on the back for the Church, saying, 'Well done, we are doing well.' It is a call for the Church to do more. Be inspired by the now-things. It is a call for you to do more.

Which of the previous chapters resonated with you? Which made you feel a little uncomfortable, excited and inspired?

Can you stand up and join Release International in the fight for the rights of the persecuted around the world?

Is peace high on your agenda? Like GreenJade, are you able to work with young people in your local community to change opinions on violence and gangs?

Do you have a heart for the poor and are you willing to sponsor a child through Compassion?

Does Authentic Media inspire you and have you the creative gifts to show something of your faith through music, art or poetry?

Are you full of hope for a brighter future? Can you stand with and support the work of Open Doors?

Are you interested in politics and, like CARE, do you want to see integrity held central among our leaders?

Were you stirred when you were led to think upon our world and the changing climate that is hurting the poor? How can you support the work of Christian Aid?

Do you always show the joy of Jesus? Did 'The Laughing Jesus' by Andy Kind ask something of your lifestyle?

These chapters excite me. These are people and organizations being the Church by representing Jesus.

Are you being Church by representing Jesus? Not your church leaders or your friends, but *you*?

To engage the mission of the Church with a local community requires you to live a never-ending personal Church life. You need to be Church.

Where does this mission come from? What inspires members of this revolutionary movement called Church to act justly and pray without ceasing? Well, a mission comes from a vision. Action comes from inspiration. So what is the vision of this revolutionary movement called Church? As Pete Greig so clearly articulated in his prayer-poem, *The Vision*: 'The vision is Jesus – obsessively, dangerously, undeniably Jesus.'

We emulate him and we are Church.

Kit Lewis
www.pentecostfestival.co.uk

APPENDIX 1
Christian Community Engagement Organizations

African Caribbean Evangelical Alliance (ACEA)
Whitefield House,
186 Kennington Park Road,
London, SE11 4BT
Tel: 02077357373

Alliance for Childhood
Kidbrooke Park,
Forest Row, RH19 5JA
Tel: (+44) 1342 822115
Email:
alliance@waldorf.compulink.co.uk

Anti-Slavery International
Thomas Clarkson House,
Broomgrove Road, London, SW9 9TL
Tel: 020 7501 8920
Web: www.antislavery.org

Aston CIU
Mayflower Centre, London, E16 1LZ
Tel: 020 7474 2255
Web:
www.astoncharities.org.uk/research

Baptist Urban Group
Baptist Church House, PO Box 44,
129 Broadway, Didcot, OX11 8RT

British Association of City Missions
47 Corpse Hill, Brighton, BN1 5GA

Christians Against Poverty (CAP)
Jubilee Mill, North Street,
Bradford, BD1 4EW
Tel: 01274 760720
Fax: 01274 760745
Web: www.capuk.org

Candl Project
Unit 2, Peterley Business Centre,
472 Hackney Road, London, E2 9EG
Tel: 020 7729 9701
Fax: 020 7728 3864
Email: candl@barnardos.org.uk

Caritas-social action
39 Eccleston Square,
London, SW1V 1BX
Tel: 020 7901 4875
Web: www.caritas@cbcew.org.uk

Catalyst Trust
Mark Perrott, 41 Tournay Road,
London SW6 7UQ
Tel: 07939 568 678
Email:mark@catalysttrust.org
Web: www.catalysttrust.org

Catholic Association for Racial Justice
9 Henry Road, Manor House,
London, N4 2LH
Tel: 020 8802 8080
Web: www.carj.co.uk

Catholic Bishops Conference of England and Wales
Richard Zipfel, Senior Policy Advisor, Dept of Christian Responsibility and Citizenship, 39 Eccleston Square, London SW1V 1BX
Tel: 020 7901 4828
Email: zipfelr@cbcew.org.uk

Christian Child Care Forum
Keith White, 10 Crescent Road, South Woodford, London, E18 1JB
www.christianchildcareforum.org.uk

Christian Ecology Link
32 Balderton Buildings, Balderton Street, London, W1Y 1TD
Tel: 020 7493 7179

Christian Socialist Movement
Andrew Bradstock, Westminster Central Hall, Storeys Gate, London, SW1H 9NH
Tel: 020 7233 3736
Email: info@thecsm.org.uk
Web: www.thecsm.org.uk

Christian Solidarity Worldwide (CSW)
PO Box 99, New Malden, Surrey, KT3 3YF

Church Action on Poverty
Central Buildings, Oldham Street, Manchester, M1 1JT
Tel: 0161 236 9321
Fax: 0161 237 5359
Web: www.church-poverty.org.uk

Church Active
Active Media Publishing Ltd, PO Box 737, Cottenham, Cambridge, CB4 8BA
Tel: 01954 206219
Email: info@echurchactive.net
Web: www.echurchactive.net

Church Army
Marlowe House, 109 Station Road, Sidcup, Kent, DA15 7AD
Web: www.churcharmy.org.uk

Church Housing Trust
Sutherland House, 70–78 West Hendon Broadway, London, NW9 7BT
Tel: 020 8202 3458
Fax 020 8202 1440

Church Urban Fund (CUF)
Church House, Great Smith Street, London, SW1P 3NZ
From February 2007 CUF are in temporary offices. Please continue to write to the address above, but check with them or their website if you want to visit.
Tel: 020 7898 1647
Email: enquiries@cuf.org.uk
Web: www.cuf.org.uk

Churches Alert to Sex Trafficking across Europe (CHASTE)
PO Box 983, Cambridge, CB3 8WY
Tel: 0845 456 9335
Email: contact@chaste.org.uk

Churches' Commission for Racial Justice (CCRJ)
3rd Floor, Bastille Court,
2 Paris Garden, London, SE1 8ND
Tel: 020 7654 7254

Churches Community Work Alliance (CCWA)
St Chad's College, North Bailey,
Durham, DH1 3RH
Tel: 0191 374 7342
Email: info@ccwa.org.uk
Web: www.ccwa.org.uk

Churches National Housing Coalition (CNHC)
Central Buildings, Oldham Street,
Manchester, M1 1JT
Tel: 0161 236 9321
Fax: 0161 237 5359

Churches Regional Network
Westminster Central Hall,
Storeys Gate, London SW1H 9NH
Tel: 020 7222 0281
Email: esimon@surfaid.org

Churches Together in Britain and Ireland
Inter-Church House, 3rd Floor,
Bastille Court, 2 Paris Garden,
London, SE1 8ND
Tel: 020 7654 7254
Email: info@ctbi.org.uk
Web: www.ctbi.org.uk

Churches Together in England
27 Tavistock Square,
London, WC1H 9HH
Tel: 020 7529 8141
Web: www.cte.org.uk

Churches Together in Wales (CYTUN)
58 Richmond Road,
Cardiff, CF24 3UR
Tel: 02920 549571
Email: post@cytun.org.uk

City Prayer networks – see World Prayer Networks

City Voices
1242 West Addison Street, Chicago,
IL 60613–3825, USA
Tel: 773 477 8163
Fax: 773 477 8394
Email: roger@cityvoice.com

Commission on Urban Life and Faith (CULF)
Report *Faithful Cities* and other findings available on: www.culf.org.uk

Community Self Build Agency
Finsbury Business Centre,
40 Bowling Green Lane,
London, EC1R 0NE
Tel: 020 7415 7092

Connections
CRE Customer Services,
PO Box 29, Norwich, NR3 1GN
Email: cre@tso.gov.uk

Children in Urban Situations
(CUrbS)
4 Hawksmoor Close, London, E6 5SL
Tel: 07941 336589
Email: info@curbsproject.org.uk
Web: www.curbsproject.org.uk

Crusaders – see Urban Saints

CUFXchange
Church Urban Fund information and
advice project.
Web: www.cufx.org.uk

Ecumenical Urban Forum
c/o Revd Andrew Davey, Church
House, Great Smith Street, London,
SW1P 3NZ

Evangelical Alliance
186 Kennington Park Road,
London, SE11 4BT
Tel: 020 7207 2100
Fax: 020 7207 2150
Email: info@eauk.org

Evangelical Coalition for Urban
Mission (ECUM)
Bethnal Green Mission,
305 Cambridge Heath Road,
London, E2 9LH
Tel: (+44) 020 7729 6262
Email: xpressanny@aol.com
Web: www.ecum.org.uk

Faithworks
Oasis Centre, 115 Southwark Bridge
Road, London, SE1 0AX
Tel: 020 7450 9000
Email: info@faithworks.info
Web: www.faithworks.info

Faith Based Regeneration
Network UK (FbRN)
9 Lambton Road, Raynes Park,
London, SW20 0LW
Tel: 020 8947 6160
Web: www.fbrn.org.uk

***Faithful Cities* Report**
Published by Commission on Urban
Life and Faith. Order from
www.chbookshop.co.uk *or*
www.mph.org.uk

Frontier Youth Trust
Unit 209f, The Big Peg,
120 Vyse Street,
Birmingham, B18 6NF
Tel: 0121 687 3505
Email: frontier@fyt.org.uk
Web: www.fyt.org.uk

Hope 2008
Ian Chisnall, Co-ordinator, 'HOPE',
Unit 4, Fairway Business Park,
Brighton, BN2 4JZ
Tel: 01273 571939
Email: ian.chisnall@hope08.com
Web: www.hope08.com

Housing Justice

Incorporating Catholic Housing Aid Society and Homelessness Sunday.
209 Old Marylebone Road,
London, NW1 5QT
Tel: 020 7723 7273
Email: info@housingjustice.org.uk
Web: www.housingjustice.org.uk

Human City Project

Human City Institute, Westhill College,
Selly Oak, Birmingham, B29 6LL

Interserve

325 Kennington Road,
London, SE11 4QH
Tel: 020 7735 8227
Email: enquiries@isewi.org

Joseph Rowntree Foundation

Web: www.jrf.org.uk

Jubilee Group

48 Northampton Road,
Croydon, CR0 7HT
Tel: 020 8656 1644
Email: vrq86@dial.pipex.com

Justice and Peace Commission

(Catholic)
National Chairperson, 116 Longhurst
Lane, Mellor, Stockport, SK6 5PG

London Institute for Contemporary Christianity

St Peter's, Vere Street,
London, W1G 0DQ
Tel: 020 7399 9555
Email: mail@licc.org.uk

Jesus in the City

(UK Urban Mission Congress)
For Congress 07: JITC Administration,
c/o Trinity College, Stoke Hill,
Bristol, BS9 1JP
Tel: 07758 520075
Email: info@jitc.org.uk
Web: www.jitc.org.uk

National Association of Christian Communities

c/o Church House,
Great Smith Street,
London, SW1P 3NZ
Tel: 020 7898 1446

National Association of Christian Communities & Networks

(NACCAN)
Community House, Eton Road,
Newport, NP19 9BL
Tel: 01633 265486

National Christian Alliance on Prostitution

PO Box 37077, London, E15 4XR
Email: ncap@ncapuk.org

National Estate Churches Network

Carole Burgess, 96 Rowsley Road,
Birmingham, B32 3PS
Tel: 0121 475 0796
Email:
adviser@nationalestatechurches.org
Web: www.nationalestatechurches.org

Nehemiah Foundation
Stephen Belling, Anthony Collins
Solicitors, 134 Edmund Street,
Birmingham, B3 2ES
Tel: 0121 212 7420
Email:
stephen.belling@anthonycollins.com

Neighbourhood Renewal
1 Seymour Terrace, Totnes,
Devon, TQ9 5AQ
Tel: 01803 863 363

Oasis Trust
15 Southwark Bridge Road,
London, SE1 0AX
Web: www:oasis.org.uk

Salvation Army
101 Newington Causeway,
London, SE1 6BN
Tel: 020 7367 4850
Email: afm@salvationarmy.org.uk

Scottish Churches Social Inclusion Network
c/o Scottish Parliamentary Office,
Scottish Storytelling Centre,
43–45 High Street,
Edinburgh, EH1 1SR
Tel: 0131 558 8137
Email: graham@acksparl.org

Set All Free
A Christian project marking 2007 as the 200th anniversary of the abolition of slave trading.
Richard Reddie, 27 Tavistock Square,
London, WC1H 9HH
Tel: 020 7529 8141
Email: infor@setallfree.net
Web: www.setallfree.net

Shaftesbury Society
16 Kingston Road,
London, SW19 1JZ
Tel: 0845 330 6033
Email:
communityinfo@shaftesburysoc.org.uk
Web: www.shaftesburysociety.org

Street Pastors
c/o The Ascension Trust,
PO Box 3916, London, SE19 1QE
Tel: 020 7771 9770
Email: ascensionswjp@yahoo.com
Web: www.streetpastors.org.uk

Tearfund
100 Church Road, Teddington,
Middlesex, TW11 8QE
Tel: 020 8239 5527
Email: wiredup@tearfund.org

UK Urban Congress Trust
– see Jesus in the City
www.jitc.org.uk

UNLOCK

Unlock House, 336a City Road,
Sheffield, S2 1GA
Tel: 0114 272 2038
Fax: 0114 276 2035
Email:office@unlock.force9.co.uk
Web: www.unlock-urban.org.uk

Urban Bishops' Panel

(Church of England)
Church House, Westminster,
London, SW1P 3NZ
Tel: 020 7898 14

Urban Bulletin

c/o ECUM, Bethnal Green Mission,
305 Cambridge Heath Road,
London, E2 9LH
Email: xpressanny@aol.com

Urban Expression

PO Box 35238, London, E1 0YA
enquire@urbanexpression.org.uk
Web: www.urbanexpression.org.uk

Urban Presence

12 Morecambe Close, Newton Heath,
Manchester, M40 2FD
Tel: 0161 688 4798
Email: derek@urbanpresence.org.uk

Urban Ministry Training Project

Partnership Building, Welbeck Road,
Newcastle upon Tyne, NE6 4JS
Tel: 0191 262 1680
Email: admin@umtp.org
Web: www.umtp.org

Urban Mission Development Advisor Project

*A joint churches and Christian agency
project encouraging networking and
joint work on urban mission.*
Web: www.urbanmission.org.uk

Urban Mission/Social Inclusion

(Baptist)
Baptist Union of Great Britain,
Baptist Church House, PO Box 44,
129 Broadway, Didcot,
Oxfordshire, OX11 9RT

The Urban Network

(Caritas-social action)
Richard Zipfel, 39 Eccleston Square,
London, SW1V 1BX
Tel: 020 7901 4875
Email: www.caritas@cbcew.org.uk

Urban Theology Unit

Christine Jones, 210 Abbeyfield Road,
Sheffield, S4 7AZ
Tel: 0114 243 5342
Fax: 0114 2435356
Email: office@utusheffield.fsnet.co.uk,
Web:
http://www.utusheffield.fsnet.co.uk

Urban Saints (formerly Crusaders)

Kestin House, 45 Crescent Road,
Luton, Beds., LU2 0AH
Tel: 01582 589850

Urban Vision

Cornerstone House, 5 Ethel Street,
Birmingham, B2 4BG
Tel: 0121 643 7771
Email:
urbanvision@mabham.globalnet.co.uk

Wired Up (e-news)

c/o Jill Clark, The Shaftesbury Society,
18 Kingston Road,
London, SW19 1JZ
Tel: 0845 330 6033
Email: wiredup@tearfund.org
Web: www.shaftesburysociety.org
(Resources section)

World Prayer Networks

(City Prayer Networks)
Cornerstone House, 5 Ethel Street,
Birmingham, B2 4BG
Web: www.worldprayer.org.uk

World Vision

599 Avebury Boulevard,
Milton Keynes, MK9 3PG
Tel: 01908 841000
Fax: 01908 841001

Worth Unlimited

Unit 209f, The Big Peg,
120 Vyse Street,
Birmingham, B18 6NF
Tel: 0121 693 5013
Email: info@worthunlimited.co.uk
Web: www.yfc.org.uk

Youth with a Mission

c/o Highfield Oval, Ambrose Lane,
Harpenden, Herts., AL5 4BX

APPENDIX 2
Prayer Resources

Following on from 'The Praying Jesus' chapter, here are some prayer-related resources:

Operation World, *21st Century edition* by Patrick Johnstone/Jason Mandryk (Authentic Media, 2005), p. 651–4

Seven Sins of England, Channel 4, May 2007

The Tide is Turning by Terry Virgo (New Wine Press, 2006), p. 7

Awake Great Britain by Wale Babatunde (Xpression Books, 2005), pp. 32–43

Why I am not a Pacifist: Faith, Christianity and Church, by C. S. Lewis (HarperCollins, 2000) pp. 281–93

A Call for Christian Leadership by John Stott (Marshalls, 1984) pp. 327–37

Living at the Edge by David Pytches (autobiography, Arcadia, 2002), p. 375

The Practice of the Presence of God and the Spiritual Maxims by Brother Lawrence (1611–91)

The Imitation of Christ by Thomas à Kempis (Penguin Books, 1952), 'The Inner Life', pp. 67–9

Enjoying Intimacy with God by J. Oswald Sanders (Moody Press, 1980)

Knowing God by J. I. Packer (Hodder & Stoughton, 1973)

The Holy Spirit: activating God's Power in your life by Billy Graham (Collins, 1978), chapter 18.

Transforming the art of leadership into the science of results by Daniel Goleman (Harvard Business School Press/Time Warner Books UK, 2002)

Impacting the City by Martin Scott, Mike Love & Sue Sinclair (Sovereign World Press, 2004), pp. 53–66

Excellence in Leadership by John White (Inter-Varsity Press, 1986) pp. 12–28

The Heavenly Man by Brother Yun (OMF Literature, 2002), chapter 20, 'The Road to Unity'

Informed Intercession by George Otis Jr (Renew Books, 1999), pp. 55–74

People in Prayer by John White (Inter-Varsity Press, 1977)

The Secret Place by Dale Fife (Whitaker House, 2001)

The Hidden Power of Prayer and Fasting by Mahesh Chavda (Destiny Image Publishers, 1998)

The Passion that Shapes Nations: catching hold of the courage of martyrs from Paul to the present by Charlie Cleverly (Kingsway Communications, 2005), pp. 7–20

The New Mystics by John Crowder (Destiny Image Publishers, 2006)

For information about the Global Day of Prayer, visit www.gdoplondon.com